THE
ARAB-
ISRAELI
CONFLICT

THE
ARAB-
ISRAELI
CONFLICT

*Other books
in the Great
Speeches
in History
series:*

THE ARAB-ISRAELI CONFLICT

GREAT SPEECHES IN HISTORY

Mark Rackers,
Book Editor

Bruce Glassman, *Vice President*

Bonnie Szumski, *Publisher*

Helen Cothran, *Managing Editor*

GREENHAVEN
PRESS®

THOMSON

GALE™

San Diego • Detroit • New York • San Francisco • Cleveland
New Haven, Conn. • Waterville, Maine • London • Munich

For more information, contact
Greenhaven Press
27500 Drake Rd.
Farmington Hills, MI 48331-3535
Or you can visit our Internet site at http://www.gale.com

LIBRARY OF CONGRESS CATALOGING-IN-PUBLICATION DATA

Arab-Israeli conflict / Mark Rackers, book editor.
    p. cm. — (Greenhaven Press's great speeches in history series)
Includes bibliographical references and index.
ISBN 0-7377-1649-5 (lib. : alk. paper)
    1. Arab-Israeli conflict. I. Rackers, Mark. II. Series.
DS119.7.A67195 2004
956.04—dc22   2003047238

Printed in the United States of America

Contents

which is much more generous than the refugee status they endure in most Arab states.

Chapter 3: The First Steps Toward Peace

1. **The Nine-Point Peace Plan**
   Abba Eban
   After its resounding victory in the Six-Day War, Israel is showing great magnanimity in being willing to negotiate at all over disputed territories. Israel is even prepared to relinquish control over sections of Jerusalem to the Arabs.

2. **Egypt Comes to Israel**
   Anwar el-Sadat
   While being stridently against the existence of Israel for more than forty years, Egypt is willing to begin talks with its neighbor. Furthermore, Egypt is willing to show its commitment to peace between the two peoples, even traveling to Jerusalem and recognizing the state of Israel's statehood.

3. **Prerequisites for Peace Accords**
   Jimmy Carter
   There are specific prerequisites for achieving peace between Israel and its Arab neighbors. First, Israel's right to exist must be recognized. Second is the establishment of permanent borders for Israel. The last requirement for peace is the creation of a Palestinian homeland.

4. **We Have Labored Long for Peace**
   Menachem Begin
   Israel welcomes a new era of peaceful existence with Egypt, the Arab world's most populous state. Israel anticipates moving forward with other Arab nations who are willing to accept Israeli statehood and work toward improved relations.

Chapter 4: The First Intifada and a Renewed Hope

Chapter 5: An Uncertain Peace

Foreword

I have a dream that one day this nation will rise up and live out the true meaning of its creed: "We hold these truths to be self-evident: that all men are created equal."

I have a dream that one day on the red hills of Georgia the sons of former slaves and the sons of former slave owners will be able to sit down together at the table of brotherhood.

I have a dream that one day even the state of Mississippi, a state sweltering with the heat of injustice, sweltering with the heat of oppression, will be transformed into an oasis of freedom and justice.

I have a dream that my four little children will one day live in a nation where they will not be judged by the color of their skin but by the content of their character.

Perhaps no speech in American history resonates as deeply as Martin Luther King Jr.'s "I Have a Dream," delivered in 1963 before a rapt audience of 250,000 on the steps of the Lincoln Memorial in Washington, D.C. Decades later, the speech still enthralls those who read or hear it, and stands as a philosophical guidepost for contemporary discourse on racism.

What distinguishes "I Have a Dream" from the hundreds of other speeches given during the civil rights era are King's eloquence, lyricism, and use of vivid metaphors to convey abstract ideas. Moreover, "I Have a Dream" serves not only as a record of history—a testimony to the racism that permeated American society during the 1960s—but it is also a historical event in its own right. King's speech, aired live on national television, marked the first time that the grave injustice of racism was fully articulated to a mass audience in a way that was both logical and evocative. Julian Bond, a fellow participant in the civil rights movement and student of King's, states that

> King's dramatic 1963 "I Have a Dream" speech before the Lincoln Memorial cemented his place as first among equals in civil rights leadership; from this first televised mass meeting, an American audience saw and heard the unedited oratory of America's finest preacher, and for the first time, a mass white audience heard the undeniable justice of black demands.

Moreover, by helping people to understand the justice of the civil rights movement's demands, King's speech helped to transform the nation. In 1964, a year after the speech was delivered, President Lyndon B. Johnson signed the Civil Rights Act, which outlawed segregation in public facilities and discrimination in employment. In 1965, Congress passed the Voting Rights Act, which forbids restrictions, such as literacy tests, that were commonly used in the South to prevent blacks from voting. King's impact on the country's laws illustrates the power of speech to bring about real change.

Greenhaven Press's Great Speeches in History series offers students an opportunity to read and study some of the greatest speeches ever delivered before an audience. Each volume traces a specific historical era, event, or theme through speeches—both famous and lesser known. An introductory essay sets the stage by presenting background and context. Then a collection of speeches follows, grouped in chapters based on chronology or theme. Each selection is preceded by a brief introduction that offers historical context, biographical information about the speaker, and analysis of the speech. A comprehensive index and an annotated table of contents help readers quickly locate material of interest, and a bibliography serves as a launching point for further research. Finally, an appendix of author biographies provides detailed background on each speaker's life and work. Taken together, the volumes in the Greenhaven Great Speeches in History series offer students vibrant illustrations of history and demonstrate the potency of the spoken word. By reading speeches in their historical context, students will be transported back in time and gain a deeper understanding of the issues that confronted people of the past.

Introduction: The History of Israel and Palestine

Thousands of years ago, the little strip of land between the river Jordan and the Mediterranean Sea was known as the land of Canaan. The Canaanites were polytheists, worshipping many gods. According to the Bible, though contested by some archaeologists and historians, around 1300 B.C. the Jews were instructed by their god Yahweh to destroy the Canaanites for their heretical beliefs and claim the land as their own.

The Jews complied and ruled the area for over five centuries under such famous kings as Saul, David, and Solomon, until they were conquered by the Assyrians from the east in 720 B.C. The Assyrians were in turn conquered, and the land was subsequently dominated by the various kingdoms of Babylon, Greece, and Rome. The Romans, it seems, were the first to introduce the moniker "Palestine" in speaking about the region. Even though the Jews were conquered and lost control of their land, they were allowed to remain in the region until the Romans destroyed Jerusalem and its temple in A.D. 70, exiling the Jewish people from the land in what became known as the Diaspora, or scattering.

Some Jews remained in the area after A.D. 70 but were very much a minority. Control of the region shifted between several different empires—the Roman, the Byzantium, the Arab, the Crusaders, and the Mamluk—until it fell to the Muslim Ottoman Empire in the 1500s and remained under their control until the twentieth century. The majority of the population was now Arab. However, being a major trade center and a crossroads between Europe, Africa, and the Far East, the area was consistently populated by a diverse mixture of peoples.

Zionism

In 1896 a journalist named Theodor Herzl published *Der Judenstaat* (*The Jewish State*). Herzl was born in Budapest but schooled in Vienna and Paris. In these European cities he experienced intense anti-Semitism, especially after the Dreyfus Affair in Paris when a Jewish officer in the French army was unjustly accused of treason. Herzl believed that assimilation of Jews into other cultures was not working. Jews, he believed, were a nation of people who needed their own state to ensure their security and command respect from the rest of the world. He slowly gained support for his cause, although many Jewish leaders dismissed him. Finally, gaining popular support and financial backing, he set up the First Zionist Congress in Basel, Switzerland, on August 29–31, 1897. The Congress declared, "Zionism seeks to establish a home for the Jewish people in Palestine secured under public law."[1] Palestine was the chosen location as it was the historical land of Israel and home to Jewish holy sites. Herzl appealed to the sultan of the Ottoman Empire who had control over the land, but was rebuked. Herzl then went to Great Britain. The British did not have influence in Palestine, but they offered the Zionists a homeland in Uganda. The Zionist Congress found this unacceptable. Without formal permission, some Jews began immigrating to Palestine and settling the land.

Then World War I erupted in 1914, and by 1918 the Ottoman Empire was destroyed. Palestine, and much of the Middle East, fell under the authority of Great Britain, one of the principal Allied victors in the war. The Jews petitioned the British government formal access to the area under the dictum: "a land without a people, for a people without a land."[2] Their petitions were granted. Jews began to immigrate en masse from all over the world to the region.

World Wars I and II

Jews flooded into the Holy Land, sometimes buying the land from the Arabs who lived there and sometimes merely claiming it as their own. Once settled, the Jewish immigrants asked the British to completely cede control of the area to the Jews.

At first the British seemed sympathetic, because in 1917 Britain had issued the Balfour Declaration. It was a brief letter expressing Britain's vague support of a Jewish homeland in Palestine but also offering support for non-Jewish peoples in the region. Many believed it was England's way of trying to buy global Jewish support for the Allied cause in World War I. Still, it was the first state recognition of the Zionist cause, though many Zionists rejected the plan, wanting immediate self-rule for any Jewish homeland. As soon as it was announced, Arabs from all the neighboring states denounced the Balfour Declaration completely. The Arabs living in Palestine also rejected the notion of a Jewish state being thrust upon the land that they had lived on for centuries. These Arabs did not have a homeland either, since the region had been claimed by Syria, Jordan, and Egypt after the Ottoman Empire fell. One of the few documents that recognized the Arab Palestinians' plight at the time was American president Woodrow Wilson's Fourteen Points—his proposal for peace after World War I, which never went into effect.

The next couple decades witnessed intense anti-Semitism across Europe and the horrors of Adolf Hitler's "final solution" in Germany—the mass extermination of 6 million Jews. During the years of World War II, Jews fled to Palestine in large numbers, most illegally as Britain had imposed strict immigration quotas. When caught, immigrants were often turned back to Europe and the very countries they were fleeing. The Jews believed that this was a barbaric injustice. Although Great Britain had promised the Jews a homeland, they were slow to give up control of the area. Palestine was located near enough to the Suez Canal to make it a strategically significant region. The Zionists became more vocal in their demands for autonomy and began conducting guerrilla attacks on British military posts inside Palestine.

Israeli Statehood

In 1947, after the war, Moshe Sharett of the Jewish Agency in Palestine addressed the newly formed United Nations, insisting, "The Jews . . . come to Palestine not to fight the Arab world, but to live at peace with it. They are not an outpost of any foreign domination. Their ambition is to integrate themselves into the modern structure of reviving Asia. They are an old Asiatic people returning to their home."[3] The United Nations voted on the Partition Plan, an agreement to divide Palestine between the Arabs and the Jews. This was not a plan to create two homelands, one for Jews and one for Palestinians, rather, some land was given to the Jews and the rest was divided between the Arab states of Syria, Jordan, and Egypt. All the Arab nations, including the Arab Palestinians, opposed the plan, not wishing to give any part of Palestine over to the Jews. But in 1948 Britain pulled their remaining troops and personnel out of the region. Shortly after, under the leadership of David Ben-Gurion, an avid Zionist and leading Israeli statesman, Israel declared its independence. The United Nations and most of the Western world, including the United States, recognized Israel, legitimizing its statehood. The neighboring Arab countries did not. The Arabs, knowing the United States and the West were clearly on the side of Israel, took advantage of the new Cold War polarity and received backing from the Soviet Union to launch an invasion of Israel. Surprising the world, the outnumbered Israelis were able to fight off their attackers and claim a victory. Thousands of Palestinian Arabs fled Israeli-held territories and became refugees in the neighboring Arab states.

The Israeli War for Independence set off the first of four major wars and countless terrorist actions that have plagued the region ever since.

Religious Claims to the Region

To understand the Arab-Israeli conflict from its beginning, one must question Israel's claim to land in Palestine. After all, the Zionists announced their right to territory that they had not controlled for over a thousand years. This had never been done before in the history of modern civilizations. Many Israelis state that the land they acquired in Palestine was virtually uninhabited and virtually uninhabitable. However, this does not account for the hundreds of thousands of Palestinian refugees that were forced to flee from the region into bordering states when Israel took over. Many Palestinians assert that the Jews are new, alien settlers in the region—

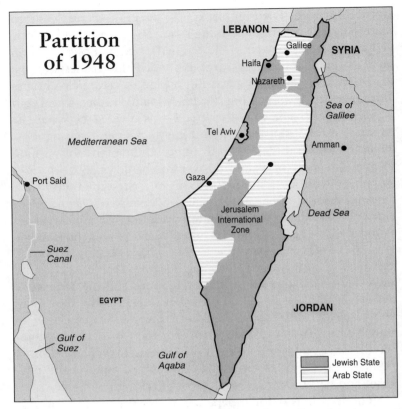

Partition of 1948

LEBANON
Galilee
SYRIA
Haifa
Nazareth
Sea of Galilee
Tel Aviv
Amman
Mediterranean Sea
Port Said
Gaza
Jerusalem International Zone
Dead Sea
Suez Canal
EGYPT
JORDAN
Gulf of Suez
Gulf of Aqaba

Jewish State
Arab State

just another wave of European colonialists. But this ignores the fact that a significant number of Jews have lived alongside Arabs in the region for thousands of years.

In fact, Palestinians and Jews share a common religious and cultural ancestry. According to the Jews, Israel was promised to Abraham by God, and the Jews are the descendants of Abraham, through his son Isaac. Muslims also trace their heritage back to Abraham, through his other son Ishmael. In fact, Muslims and Jews believe in the same one God. In Judaism, he is Yahweh. Yahweh, translated into Arabic, is Allah. Jews are Semitic people as are the Palestinians and all Arabs.

Palestinians have argued that they could clearly not be anti-Semitic and have never been anti-Jewish. They insist they have only been anti-Zionist. Further, they never committed genocide on the Jewish people. Palestinians wonder why they should be made to suffer and give up their land to create a homeland for Jews. Why not Germany? But the Jews insisted on the Holy Land, claiming it as an ancestral homeland.

The Jews, however, did lose control of the region in the first century. Since then, the ethnic character of the region changed. Muhammad, the founding prophet of Islam, was born in A.D. 570. By the seventh century, Islam had spread across the Middle East. In A.D. 691, Muslims built the Dome of the Rock on the ruins of the Jewish king Solomon's Temple in Jerusalem. The Dome of the Rock, coupled with the al-Aqsa Mosque, forms Islam's third holiest site, after Mecca and Medina. Muslims believe it is the spot where Muhammad rose into heaven. And according to Muslims, while it is true and respected that the Jews were there first, Muhammad is the last prophet, the last to receive God's revelations; therefore, he and his followers have the most legitimate claim to the land. The site of the ruined temple, however, also includes the Western Wall, the most sacred place of worship for Jews. Despite the recent Muslim structures, Jews still consider Jerusalem to be a Jewish holy city—one they do not intend to relinquish willingly. Because of this, Jerusalem remains the most contentious of the disputed holy sites in the region. Edward Said, the Palestinian scholar writes:

> Beginning with Judaism and Christianity, each is a successor haunted by what came before; for Muslims, Islam fulfills and ends the line of prophecy. There is still no decent history or demystification of the many-sided contest among these three followers—not one of them by any means a monolithic, unified camp—of the most jealous of all gods, even though the bloody modern convergence on Palestine furnishes a rich secular instance of what has been so tragically irreconcilable about them.[4]

The Separation Persists

If Israel was a new phenomenon in the Middle East, so were other Arab nations. After World War I the European powers, notably Great Britain and France, tried to further their own colonial interests. For example, Iraq was formed by combining several separate kingdoms into one huge Arab state, under puppet leadership that took orders from the European nations. Older kingdoms such as Egypt, Syria, and Jordan tried to extend their borders and capture new territory. After World War II and continuing into the decades that followed, there was a further realignment of power. The countries still under control of the French and British began to kick off the yoke of imperialism and claim ownership of land.

However, even with all these shifting borders, there was still no such thing as a Palestinian nation. Israel often points to this, noting the fallacy of claiming the Jews stole a country away from the Palestinians. The Palestinians never had one. They were usually considered part of southern Syria or western Jordan, but not because they desired to be. It is true the Israelis refused to cede their small slice of land to the Palestinians (Israel did not even have control of Jerusalem at this time). It is also true the Arab countries refused to do so as well. The surrounding Arab nations wanted control of all the land claimed by the Palestinians and the Israelis. Israel constantly found itself fighting for survival against these Arab nations, first in their War for Independence, then again in the 1950s.

In 1952 King Farouk of Egypt was overthrown by Gamal Abdel Nasser. Nasser was fervently anti-imperialist. He believed the king was a puppet of the West, and he saw Israel as merely another example of European colonialism. He nationalized the Suez Canal (which had been under the control of several European powers). He allowed the fedayeen, anti-Israeli terrorists, to be trained on Egyptian soil and he enlisted the support of Syria and Jordan as allies in challenging Israeli sovereignty. Israel felt squeezed. At the same time, Great Britain wished to regain its control of the vital Suez Canal. With England and France backing the effort, Israel launched an attack against Egypt on October 29, 1956, and quickly captured the Sinai Peninsula. Most world leaders condemned the war. Under intense pressure from both the United States and the Soviet Union, England and France pulled out and Israel withdrew from the territory it gained.

The PLO and the Six-Day War

In 1964 the Palestine Liberation Organization (PLO) was formed, trained, and supported by Egypt and Nasser's government. Under its first leader, Ahmad Al-Shuqairi, it claimed that it was the first organization speaking directly for the Palestinian people. Many accused it of existing as merely a tool of terror for Nasser to promote his visions of Arab nationalism. Echoing Nasser's own stated views, the PLO charter decried the state of Israel and promoted its destruction. The PLO waged a guerrilla war on Israel throughout the 1960s. Those supporting the PLO considered its members as freedom fighters. Israel, and much of the world, considered them terrorists who indiscriminately targeted military and civilian targets alike. Israel was not the only target of PLO attacks. The organization turned some of its rancor on Jordan and Syria, which maintained their rights to Palestinian land in the West Bank and Golan Heights, respectively.

However, Jordan's position seemed the most generous. It had been the only Arab nation to offer Palestinians full citizenship, even proposing to blanket them and their territory of the West Bank under one united kingdom of Jordan and Palestine. The West Bank was the area of land west of Jordan, literally extending from the west bank of the Jordan River and the Dead Sea and containing the major cities and holy sites of Jerusalem, Ramallah, Jericho, and Bethlehem. Jordan's offer was not well received. It was clear the Palestinians were no longer interested in being absorbed or ruled under any government other than one of their own creation.

In 1967 Egypt mobilized its military forces on the border with Israel. Nasser enlisted the support of Syria, Iraq, this time a reluctant Jordan, and the new PLO for what was to be the final destruction of Israel. But on June 5, 1967, Yitzhak Rabin, the Israeli army chief of staff, ordered a preemptive strike, taking the Arab forces by surprise. Israel was able to destroy nearly the entire Egyptian air force before it even left the ground. Within six days, Israel conquered the other Arab armies and captured land all around its borders. By the time the UN brokered a cease-fire, Egypt lost the Sinai Peninsula, Jordan lost the West Bank, including Jerusalem, and Syria lost their prized Golan Heights. This was a huge victory for Israel, both militarily and psychologically. It was evident they were a force to be reckoned with, cementing their place in the region and more than doubling their size. The capture of

Jerusalem meant that the Jewish holy sites were once again under Jewish control after a millennium.

Shortly after the war in 1967, the United Nations passed Resolution 242. It called upon Israel to relinquish all territories it gained in the war. It also called for a fair treatment of refugees and for all the Arab states to recognize Israel's right to exist. However, the resolution lacked real teeth. The Arab states were not willing to recognize Israel as a state. Israel was not willing to relinquish land it felt it acquired justly in a defensive war. Israeli leaders felt that the land was critical in creating security buffers between itself and its belligerent neighbors. Finally, while respecting the borders of all states in the region, the resolution fell short of recommending a Palestinian state, which was unacceptable to the PLO and its new charismatic leader, Yasser Arafat.

The situation remained incredibly tense in the region. In 1970 Anwar el-Sadat, Nasser's successor as the new leader of Egypt, commented on Israel, "Don't ask me to make diplomatic relations with them. Never. Never. Leave it to the coming generations to decide that, not me."[5] In 1973 Syria and Egypt launched a strike deep into Israel as Jews observed the holiday of Yom Kippur. Israel quickly repelled the invading forces but it proved a psychological victory for the Arabs, providing them a retaliatory blow for the Six-Day War. The United Nations felt compelled to negotiate peace in the region. It allowed Yasser Arafat, the leader of the PLO, to address the General Assembly, a first for a Palestinian. He brought a gun and an olive branch, and rhetorically challenged the world to decide which path the Palestinians should choose, more violence or peace. While invoking the olive branch, the symbol of peace, it was clear that Arafat did not envision a Palestinian state alongside an Israeli state, but one that replaced it. Israel refused to recognize PLO authority in the negotiations. The United States threatened to do likewise unless the PLO would openly recognize UN Security Council Resolution 242 and Israel's right to exist. Under pressure from Palestinian hard-liners, Arafat and the PLO refused.

In 1977 Anwar el-Sadat shocked the world by stating he was willing to "go to the ends of the earth" to achieve peace in the region. Israel responded immediately and invited Sadat to

Jerusalem to speak to Israel's Knesset. Addressing their parliament, Sadat stated, "I go back to the question, 'how can we achieve this doable peace?' In my mind we can declare it here, before the whole world, the answer is neither difficult nor is it impossible despite long years of fear, blood, vengeance, spite and hatred and generations of hostility. The answer is not difficult nor impossible if we act sincerely and faithfully."[6] In agreeing to travel to Israel, Sadat became the first Arab leader to recognize Israel as a state. U.S. president Jimmy Carter volunteered to mediate a peace agreement between Egypt and Israel at Camp David. Close to two years later, Sadat and Israeli prime minister Menachem Begin signed the Camp David Accords, winning each of them the Nobel Peace Prize. Egypt, the Jews' largest and oldest enemy, and Israel agreed to permanent peace. Israel gave back the Sinai Peninsula, uprooting many settlements there that had prospered since the Six-Day War, and the United States agreed to give financial aid to both countries.

While the world cheered, thinking the Arab-Israeli conflict was close to resolution, several factors quickly cast doubts on long-term peace. The 1980s were turbulent. Sadat, whose accords with Israel angered many Arab nations, was assassinated. And while Israel was willing to give up the Sinai Peninsula, it seemed unwilling to give up other territories acquired during the Six-Day War. It claimed the whole of Jerusalem as its everlasting capital, annexed the Golan Heights, created settlements in the West Bank and invaded Lebanon, which had always been a somewhat neutral player in the area. Israel claimed this attack was necessary, stating that Lebanese land was needed as protection from continued strikes in the north, where Syrian-backed forces were based.

This move led to further bloodshed. New terrorist groups formed, like Hizballah in southern Lebanon, creating new fronts against Israel. In 1987 the Palestinians launched an intifada, or popular uprising, in the West Bank and Gaza Strip in response to continued Israeli occupation. Palestinians from all walks of life took to the streets in protest. They refused to pay taxes to Israel. Many quit their jobs in Israeli-owned businesses. At the same time, Jordan finally relinquished its claims over the West Bank to the Palestinians. Israel used its military to control the intifada. The use of force was not good public relations. While most nations were still sympathetic to the Jewish state, they abhorred the heavy-handed tactics it used in trying to quell the protests. Images of tanks rolling over homes and chasing down Palestinian children appeared on the nightly news worldwide.

The Gulf War in 1990 diverted much attention away from the problem in Israel, at least for a short time. Unknown to the world, Israel and the Palestinians had been conducting secret meetings in Oslo, Norway. In 1993 it was announced that some tentative headway had been reached. At the time, Arafat stated, "Our two peoples are awaiting today this historic hope and they want to give peace a real chance."[7] Israel and the PLO signed an agreement, providing mutual recognition between the two parties, giving the Palestinians limited self-rule in the Gaza Strip and the West Bank and a promise of a final settlement in the future. The next year, Israel signed an agreement with Jordan, guaranteeing peace and establishing agreements on water rights—which had been a contested issue between the two countries for decades.

Peace Hangs in the Balance

The Oslo Accords seemed to be sticking. Then, in 1995, Israel's Prime Minister Yitzhak Rabin was assassinated by a Jewish extremist. Rabin, the hawk from the Six-Day War, had become one of the greatest advocates for peace with the Palestinians. In his last speech he spoke of the peace process, "This is a course which is fraught with difficulties and pain. For Israel, there is no path that is without pain. But the path of peace is preferable to the path of war."[8] When he died, Israel voted in the more conservative Benjamin Netanyahu. The peace process slowed considerably. Still, there was movement. The Palestinians elected the Palestinian National Authority (PNA) as its ruling body under Arafat, and more sections of the Gaza Strip and the West Bank fell under their authority.

Into the Twenty-first Century

Then, in late 2000 and early 2001 violence erupted again, born from a handful of events. First, there was a deadline set by Oslo for a final accord. This was not met. Second, the soon-to-be prime minister Ariel Sharon visited Jerusalem's Temple Mount to stress Israel's claim to the site. Since the location also contains an important Islamic holy site, Muslims were infuriated. Then, Yasser Arafat made a speech at the World Economic Forum in January 2001. The Israeli prime minister at that time, Ehud Barak, had been working with U.S. president Bill Clinton and chief Palestinian negotiator Abu Mazen (Mahmoud Abbas) on furthering the peace process. Many thought that they were very close to a deal that ensured Palestinian sovereignty and Israeli security. At the World Economic Forum, the Israelis took the stage, praising the Palestinians and the peace process. Arafat followed and lambasted his Israeli counterparts for waging a "savage and barbaric war" against the Palestinians, accusing Israel of using ammunitions containing depleted uranium and demanding Israel live up to the age-old UN Resolution 242, which had never been fully implemented. He asked the audience, "Have you seen a more ugly policy than this policy of collective punishment or more destruction in the contemporary age?"[9] The Israelis felt insulted and did not respond. All peace talks were suspended. A second intifada broke out. Israel blamed Arafat, saying this was not a popular uprising like the one seen a decade before but a deliberate use of terror against Israel to pressure them to give away land, and Israel swore it would not negotiate with terrorists.

In June 2002, U.S. president George W. Bush pushed the PLO to arrange new leadership for the Palestinian National Authority. This bitter pill was sugarcoated with an American commitment to the creation of an independent Palestine. Arafat and the PLO agreed to the implied "deal" and appointed Abu Mazen as the new prime minister of the PNA in April 2003. While Mazen took office, the United States, Russia, the European Union, and the United Nations put forward a "road map" for peace in the region that both Israel and the Palestinian Authority were to follow. Both sides tentatively agreed to follow the plan; however, the U.S.-led invasion of Iraq in March assumed the national spotlight, allowing the Israelis and the Palestinians to let the road map languish. In September 2003, Mazen resigned as prime min-

26

ister over differences with Yasser Arafat. His successor, Abu Ala (Ahmed Qurei) has pledged to resume the peace process by following—along with the Israelis—the UN road map. Only small steps have been taken along the road, and no one is sure that this map will lead to lasting peace in the region. Since the beginning of the second intifada, thousands have died on all sides of this conflict. Tensions in the region have continued to flare as they have for nearly a century, sometimes with weapons, sometimes with words. Speeches provide an interesting window, a way to glimpse the personalities that have shaped this struggle. The speeches in this anthology try to trace the history of the Arab-Israeli conflict from the points of view of the warriors and the peacemakers. Some let readers see the pain that has ignited so much hatred and death, and some offer a sense of hope that perhaps this conflict will not engulf the century to come.

Notes

1. Quoted in "Theodor (Binyamin Ze'ev) Herzl (1860–1904)," Jewish Virtual Library, 2003. www.us-israel.org.

2. Quoted in H.E. Gaafar Allagany, 1992 UN speech on Item 35: the situation in the Middle East, Royal Embassy of Saudi Arabia. www.saudiembassy.net.

3. Moshe Sharett, address to the General Assembly of the United Nations on May 12, 1947, Israel's Ministry of Foreign Affairs. www.mfa.gov.

4. Edward Said, "Clash of Ignorance," Nation, October 22, 2001.

5. Anwar el-Sadat, address to the U.S. Congress on November 5, 1975, History Channel.com. http://historychannel.com.

6. Anwar el-Sadat, address to Israeli parliament on November 20, 1977. History Channel.com. http://historychannel.com.

7. Yasser Arafat, speech on the first Israeli-Palestinian peace agreement, History Channel.com. http://historychannel.com.

8. Yitzhak Rabin, Yitzhak Rabin's last speech, Tel Aviv Plaza Hotel, 1995, Ariga.com. http://ariga.com.

9. Yasser Arafat, speech at the World Economic Forum in Davos on January 28, 2001, PLO Negotiations Affairs Department. www.nad-plo.org.

GREAT
SPEECHES
IN
HISTORY

Establishing a Jewish State

We Will Not Abandon Zion

David Ben-Gurion

David Ben-Gurion, considered the founding father of Israel, would solidify his place in history on May 14, 1948 when he announced the birth of Israel. Before becoming prime minister of the new Jewish state, Ben-Gurion (born David Gruen) worked doggedly for many years toward the Zionist cause of creating a Jewish homeland, as is witnessed in this speech in January of 1946 to the Anglo-American Committee of Enquiry. This committee was comprised of six British and six American members. It held hearings and heard proposals from Jews and Arabs in response to the question of Jewish immigration to Palestine.

At the time, the majority of land in the Middle East, including Palestine, was under the control of the British Empire (and to a lesser extent, France). The world was reeling from the devastation of World War II and was just beginning to understand the scope of Hitler's "final solution." Ben-Gurion outlines the long history of Jewish persecution, from being driven out of their homeland thousands of years ago, to their marginalization and persecution throughout Europe, to the extermination of Jews under the Third Reich. Ben-Gurion insists that Jews intend to work with Palestinians in creating their new homeland, and to use only the land that the Palestinians have no use for. He claims the Jewish people have a right of ownership to the land; a right that dates back thousands of years. He also stresses the importance of Zion, and dismisses the notion that it is only a mystical or spiritual place.

David Ben-Gurion, *Rebirth and Destiny of Israel*, edited and translated by Mordekhai Nurock. New York: Philosophical Library, 1954.

The Committee of Enquiry unanimously recommended the admittance of Jews to Palestine but could not
agree on the future of Palestinians who would likely be
displaced. It also stopped short of recommending either a
Jewish or Arab state, but suggested a jointly controlled
state that would restrict Jewish immigration to maintain
a balance in the region. Frustrated at this measure, Ben-
Gurion increased Jewish immigration from Europe to
Palestine, exceeding the limits placed by the committee.

Sir, our case seems to us simple and compelling. It rests
on two elementary principles. One is that we Jews are
just like other human beings, entitled to just the same
rights; that the Jewish people is entitled to the same equality
of treatment as any free and independent people in the
world. The second is that this is and will remain our country.
We are here as of right. We are not here on the strength of
the Balfour Declaration[1] or of the Palestine Mandate.[2] We
were here long, long before. I myself was. Many thousands
preceded me, but we were here far earlier still. Speaking from
the legal point of view, it is the Mandatory Power that is here
on the strength of the Mandate. Our case, and I think you
will meet many such now in Europe, is that of one who
builds a house for his family to live in and is evicted forcibly
and the house given to somebody else. It changes hands and
the owner returns and wants to get it back. In many cases the
Jew is kept out, it is occupied by that other tenant. To be
more exact I will put it this way. It is a large building, this
building of ours, with, say, 150 rooms. We were expelled
from it and our family was scattered. Somebody else took the
building away and again it changed hands many times, and
then we came back at last and found some five rooms occupied by other people, the other rooms destroyed and unin-

1. Although this British declaration issued on November 2, 1917 did regard Palestine, the proposals of the declaration were vague. Zionists, however, interpreted
its mandates as giving them claim to the region. 2. Issued at the end of World War I,
this mandate effectively gave control over Palestine to the British government. The
British then gave Jews the right to settle in the region.

habitable from neglect. We said to the occupants: 'We do not
want to dispossess you, please stay where you are, we are going back to these uninhabitable rooms, we will repair them.'
And we did repair some of them and settled there. Now some
other members of our family are coming back and want to
repair some other of the uninhabitable rooms. But the occupants say: 'No, we are here, we do not want you, we do not
live in these rooms, they are no good for any human being,
but we do not want to repair them or make them better.' And
again we do not say to them: 'Depart, it is all ours.' We say:
'You stay, you are there, if only since yesterday, you may stay
if you please and we will help you repair your rooms too if
you wish; if not you can do so yourselves.' At hand there are
many big buildings, half empty. We do not say to them:
'Please move over to that other big building.' No, we say:
'Please stay here, we will be good neighbors.'. . .

A History of Discrimination

What I am going to do is simply to tell you what we Jews are
in our own country, who we are, what we are doing, what we
are aiming at. Why are we here, and for what? Perhaps that
will explain things.

There are now some 600,000 of us, more than one-third
born in the country, some families here for many centuries,
and not living in the towns only. There are Jewish fellahin,
peasants who have stayed put for hundreds of years; they live
in Ramleh and in Galilee. But the majority of us were not
born here; I was not. We have come from all parts of the
world, and from all countries. Not only where Jews were
persecuted physically, exterminated or repressed as they were
in Nazi Germany and Poland, in the Yemen and in Morocco,
in Czarist Russia, Persia and Fascist Italy. Many of us are
from free countries where Jews were treated as citizens,
where persecution was not—Britain, the United States of
America, Canada and the Argentine, pre-war Imperial Germany, Soviet Russia, France, Egypt and elsewhere. Why did
we come? What is the common denominator which brought
us all here? Let me tell you.

First it was escape from dependence and discrimination. I

do not mean from anti-semitism. There was a great deal of talk in your Commission about anti-semitism and many of our people were asked to explain why it is. But it is not for us to answer. It is your baby, it is a Christian baby. It is for you Gentiles to explain. Perhaps we ought to set up a Jewish Commission to make an enquiry of the Gentiles, or perhaps a joint Jewish-Gentile Commission, with one Chairman Jewish and one Gentile, to interrogate leaders of the Church, teachers, educators, journalists and political parties on what this disease is, and what the reason for it in the Gentile world. . . . But I am not concerned with anti-semitism; as I say, it is not our business. I am concerned with why Jews have come here. They came because they felt it unendurable for many of them to be at the mercy of others. Sometimes those others are excellent people but not invariably, and you have discrimination. It need not be legal or political or economic discrimination; at times it is merely a moral one and, as human beings with human dignity, they do not like it. No, they do not like it, yet they do not see how they can change the whole world.

You ask me what is moral discrimination. Gentlemen, I do not know in Europe a more tolerant, a more liberal, a more fair-minded people than the English in their own country; perhaps the Scandinavian peoples are like that too, but I do not know them as well as I know the British, although I do not claim to know the British fully. I do not think anyone can claim that except the British themselves, if indeed they can. Recently in the House of Lords, one of the noblest institutions in the world, whatever one may think of it from the democratic angle, there was a debate on the Jewish question. Only in England, I believe, could you have such a debate. In it the Archbishop of York in very strong language condemned anti-semitism as unchristian. Coming from His Grace that means a lot—unchristian. Practically it may not help us very much, but we appreciate it very deeply as a moral aid. He then began talking about the Jewish criticism of the policy of His Majesty's Government in Palestine, meaning the White Paper of 1939,[3] and the attack launched

---

3. The White Paper of 1939, issued by the British government, called for restrictions on Jewish immigration and called for an independent Palestinian state. It was rejected by both Jews and Arabs.

against it by Jews on both sides of the Atlantic, and he said these significant words: '(Such criticism) is being resented and may easily lead to a most dangerous reaction.'

Well, Jews are not the only people who criticize or attack the White Paper. In 1939 it was described, not by a Jew, but by an Englishman, a pure Englishman, a Gentile, as a mortal blow to the Jewish people. His name, Gentlemen, is Winston Churchill.

Persecution

We agree with his description. It was and is a mortal blow. Well, Gentlemen, when a people is dealt a mortal blow, who would ask it to lie down and take it dumbly? Who should resent this criticism, this attack on a mortal blow? And in 1939 when our people in Europe were still alive! Since then tens of thousands of human beings, of babies—after all, Jewish babies are also babies—have had to perish. Because of that blow they could not be saved. I do not suggest that all found death because of it, but tens of thousands could have been saved, yet were not—because of it. Is it surprising that we, as human beings, should criticise or attack it? I am sure His Grace understands that. He is a great personality, but he knows the mind of his people and he said it may lead to a most dangerous reaction. That is what I call moral discrimination. We receive a deadly thrust; we must be silent. Else there may be trouble for us. Where? Not in Poland, but in the most liberal and tolerant country, I say it with the greatest respect, in England. Why discrimination? There are many Jews who submitted to it; there are some who refused to submit, and that is what brought them over here. There they were at the mercy of nice people, but nice people may sometimes become very nasty, when they have the power and are dealing with a minority. Why is there this discrimination? As I see it, it is for two reasons: because we happen to be different from others, and we happen to be a minority. We are not the only people who are different from others: and in truth we are not different at all, for difference is a term of relativity. If there was only one person in the world, he would not be 'different'. We are—what we are. Others are different, but, as they

see us, it is we who are. But we are what we are and we like
to be what we are. Is that a crime? Cannot a man be what he
is? Cannot a people be what it is? On the continent I know
they consider the British very different, and so they are; but
no Englishman will think himself different. He is, but he is
not different; he is just what he is and we are too: we are just
what we are. We happen to be different because other people
are different. For that, our people suffers. The English do not
suffer because they are different. On the contrary, for them it
is a great compliment, a great strength. They have their own
individuality and people are brought to respect it. As for us,
not only are we different, we are in a minority. We are at the
mercy of others, in that people do not like us being different.
It becomes very hazardous sometimes for us, because other
people want us to be like them and from time to time to renounce either our nationhood or our religion or our country
or our language. Many of us made the renunciation—not all,
but some of us, and still do. You have perhaps met some
such. The Jewish people as a whole defies any superior material power that asks us to surrender spiritual values which
are dear to us and are ours. And we pay the price, sometimes
a very high price, for sticking to our spiritual principles.

It is a long story. It goes back 2,300 years, to when the
known world, Egypt, Syria and Persia, became Hellenized.
Judea did not bow to that higher culture—for it was in many
respects a higher one; the Jews preferred to be just what they
were. So they suffered. There was another clash when Rome
became the dominant power, and we were asked to accept the
divinity of the Caesars, and again we refused. Here were the
most mighty rulers of the world, above all other men, and recognized divine, but not by us. So again we suffered and fought
and were foiled, but not in spirit. We defied the material
power. Then it happened again with the rise of Christianity. I
must be careful what I say. The whole of Europe was con-
verted to Christianity, many by force. We stood out, though
we perhaps had more to do with it than other peoples; for St.
Paul was a Jew. We refused, and we paid the price. We are still
paying it, and it is a very high one. I read the evidence of some
Moslems and I felt that what came with Christianity recurred
with the rise of another great religion. I will say no more.

Then the French Revolution asked us to give up our nationhood. Some Jews did, but not the Jewish people. And now this last phase [i.e., the Holocaust]. I am not going to speak about it. What happened in the last few years is unspeakable. Why should I harrow you with Jewish sentiments? It happened to us, and to no one else. I will tell you only of one emotion I experienced when I knew of what had taken place: it was this—at least I and my children are happy that we belong to a people that is being slaughtered and not to those who are slaughtering us, nor to those who look on with indifference. I know many Christians in France, in Holland, in Belgium and other countries who risked their lives to save a Jew or a Jewish child. We will never forget that—never. But there were other things, not things that happened in Nazi Europe, which are outside the pale of humanity; I am not discussing them. There was a conspiracy of silence in the entire world. When we suffered and tried to tell you of our sufferings, the answer was: it is Jewish propaganda, just Press publicity of the Jews. I merely ask myself—would you suffer if a million Gentile babies were slaughtered in Europe? . . .

Why are we tortured? Why these subterfuges to lock up that hapless fragment of Polish Jewry? Some 30,000 Jews remain in Poland out of three millions, and every day they are massacred. Why imprison them? They are human beings. Why this discrimination in your Christendom? Why must we wait, why cannot we escape from this dependence, this being at the beck of others?

That is one reason why we want to get back here, and there is a second. It is love of Zion, a deep love, passionate and undying. It is unique, but a fact; you will see it here. There are 600,000 of us here because of it.

Love of Zion

In evidence given to you in America, an American Arab, I believe it was John Hassan, said no Palestine was ever known as a political and geographical entity; and another American Arab, a great Arab historian, Dr. Hitti, went even further and said, and I am quoting him: 'There is no such thing as Palestine in history, absolutely not.' And I agree with him entirely;

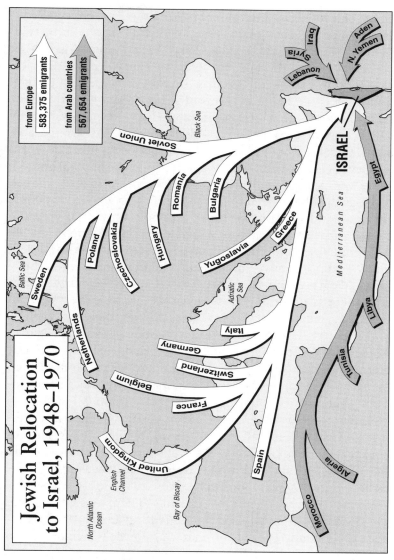

Jewish Relocation to Israel, 1948–1970

from Europe
583,375 emigrants

from Arab countries
567,654 emigrants

but when he speaks of history he means Arab history, he is a specialist in that and knows his business. In Arab history there is indeed no such thing as Palestine. Arab history was made in Arabia, Syria and Persia, in Spain and North Africa. You will not find Palestine in it. There is, however, something more than Arab history; there is world history and Jewish history and in that history there is a country named Judea, or as we call it Eretz Israel, the Land of Israel. We have called it Israel since the days of Joshua. There was such a country in history, there was indeed, and it is still there. It is a little country, a very little one, but it made a very deep impression on world history—and on ours, because it made us a people: and our people made it. No other people in the world made it; it made no other people. It entered world history by way of many wars, of Egyptians, Babylonians, Assyrians, Persians, Greeks, Romans, Byzantines. It gained a place in world history, because in it our people created perhaps a limited, but a very great, civilization, and here the Jews were shaped to be as they have been until this day: a very exclusive people on one hand and on the other a people universal; very national and very international. Exclusive in their internal life and attachment to their history, to their national and religious tradition; universal in their religious, social and ethical ideas. We were told that there is one God in the entire world, that there is unity of the human race because every human being was created in the image of God, that there ought to be and there will be brotherhood and social justice on earth, peace between peoples. Those were our ideas; this was our culture and this made history here. Here we created a Book, many books. Some were lost, some survived only in translations, but twenty-four remain in their original language—Hebrew, the language, Mr. Chairman, in which I am thinking now as I talk to you in English, and which the Jews in this country are speaking now. We went into exile, but we took that Book with us, and in that Book—which was more to us than a Book, it was our very selves—we took with us our country in our hearts and in our souls. These three, the Land, the Book and the People, are for us forever one. It is an indissoluble bond. There is no material power which can undo it, only our physical destruction can. . . .

Somebody may tell you: 'All this is merely a mystical attachment to a mystical Zion, not to this physical Zion.' But now you will see 600,000 living human beings whom the love of Zion has brought here and kept here. They are attached to the living Zion, although it has for them a profound spiritual significance as well.

Then we are asked what seems a very common-place

question: 'When the Arabs conquered Spain, did they not create a magnificent civilization there?' Yes, they did. They created it and then were driven out. Can they claim Spain for the Arabs? Have they a right to Spain? I know of no retort which proves our case so forcibly as this, and I take it up. Is there a single Arab in the entire world who dreams about Spain? Is there an Arab in Iraq or in Egypt or anywhere who knows the rivers and mountains of Spain more than he knows his present country? Is there an Arab in the world who will give his money to Spain? What is Spain to him? . . .

Here are Jews who have been parted for centuries, some of them for many centuries, some of them for thousands of years like the Jews in Yemen, yet they have always carried Zion in their hearts, and finally came back, and came back with love. Where in the world will you find people loving their country as the Jews love Zion? . . .

A Jewish State

There was a third reason for our coming, and it is the crux of the problem. We came here with an urge for Jewish independence, for what you call a Jewish State. When people in the world outside talk about a State, it means power, domination. For us it means other.

We came here to be free Jews. I mean in the full sense of the word, 100 percent free and 100 percent Jews, and that we could not be anywhere else—not Jews, free. We believe we are entitled to be Jews, to live a full Jewish life as an Englishman lives his English life and an American lives his, and to be free from fear and dependence, no longer to be objects of pity and sympathy, of philanthropy and 'justice,' in the eyes of others. We believe that is our due, both as individuals and as a people. . . .

Freedom begins at home, in man's mind and spirit, and here we have built our Jewish freedom more securely than any other Jews in the world. Why do we feel freer than other Jews? It is because we are self-made Jews, made by our country and making it. We are a Jewish community which is, in fact, a Jewish Commonwealth in the making. . . .

A Jewish State means Jewish security. If there is one thing a Jew lacks everywhere in the world it is security, and after all he is entitled to feel secure. Why the lack? Because, even if he is safe, he is not safe of himself. Somebody else provides for his security. Well, we want to provide for our own security, and we have been doing it here from the start.

I came to Palestine 40 years ago and I went to work in Sejera, a little village in Galilee. I had never before been a worker or a farmer and I had to learn two things at once, how to hold a plow in my hands and how a rifle. I had to provide for my security, for the security of the village, and I went to work in the fields with a rifle on my shoulder. We had a special organization to keep watch. There were very few watchmen, and from time to time they were attacked. When I stood watch in the long nights and lifted up mine eyes, I understood the magnificence of the full meaning of the words in the Book of Solomon, that the heavens tell the glory of God.

We tried to make friends with our neighbors. It was not easy. I do not know what their reasons were for attacking us. They sometimes attacked others too, but us a little more. They have a great contempt for people who are afraid. They learned to know we were not like that, that we could take care of ourselves, and so they respected us, and we did our best to win their friendship and often succeeded. We are still doing our level best all the time in all our settlements, to maintain decent human relations with them. But we have had to look after ourselves. We held on to our weapons, but never used them save for self-defense. . . .

We are striving to build up a new society, a free society based on justice, on human justice, and on the highest human intellectual and moral endeavor. If you find time to visit our agricultural settlement, you will see something of that spirit there. We seek also to help solve the tragic problem, the great historic dilemma, of the Jewish people throughout the world. Because, Sir, only a Jewish State can build a Jewish National Home. We need the State in order to continue building that National Home, for those Jews who for one reason or another, even if their fate be death, will be impelled to come just as we came; only the Jewish State can do it. . . .

We Will Not Give Up

There is tension at the moment, perhaps a little more than tension, between us and the Arabs. It is very unfortunate. But it is transient. It is not a danger. We may be of great help to them as they to us. I believe we need each other. We have something to offer each other as equals, but only as equals. No people in the world can stand alone, whether it be a small nation or a great Power. There is an interdependence of peoples, and in that sense we too need to be dependent, as Belgium is, as are Sweden and Norway. Norway is the best example for us in many ways. They have something in common with us there, in human and social perceptions.

There will be not only peace between us and the Arabs, there will be alliance, there will be friendship. It is an historical necessity, just as much as is a Jewish State. It is a moral, a political and an economic necessity.

We are here as of right. We will not abandon Zion, as we never abandoned a Jewish imperative, whatever the price may be; and we will not abandon a Jewish Commonwealth. . . .

There are things that to us are dearer than our lives, and we love life. The Jewish religion was never an ascetic religion; we do not despise life—we cherish it. We are not going to give up, even if we have to pay a heavy toll, and there are hundreds of thousands of Jews, here and in other lands, who will give up their lives, if they must, for Jewish independence and for Zion.

Palestine Offers Peace or Armed Resistance

Yasser Arafat

Yasser Arafat has been a central figure in the fight for
Palestinian autonomy since the 1950s and was elected
chairman of the Palestine Liberation Organization (PLO)
in 1969. In this speech, given in 1974, he makes a plea
directly to the United Nations General Assembly for
Palestinian self-determination. While earlier, Arafat was
an advocate of guerilla warfare against Israel, in this
speech he seems to make a dramatic turn toward peace.

   This speech, which was one of the first times Palestinians were allowed to speak for themselves on the
world stage, advances a very different story of the region.
Israeli diplomats tended to assert that the land they were
awarded by the Partition Plan of 1948 was 75 percent
uninhabited desert. Arafat calls this way of thinking a
myth and continually articulates the history of a Palestinian presence in the area. He likens his fight to the many
"freedom-fighters" around the world and desires the
same support the UN has shown post-colonial states in
Africa, Asia, and South America. At the end of his speech
he makes the famous powerful statement, "Today I have
come bearing an olive branch and a freedom-fighter's
gun. Do not let the olive branch fall from my hand."

   While invoking the olive branch, the symbol of
peace, it is clear that Arafat does not envision a Palestinian state alongside an Israeli state, but one that replaces

Yasser Arafat, address to the United Nations, November 13, 1974.

it. For this reason, Israel refused to recognize PLO authority in these negotiations. The United States threatened to do likewise unless the PLO would openly recognize UN Security Council resolution 242 of 1967 and Israel's right to exist. Under pressure from Palestinian hardliners, Arafat and the PLO refused.

Mr. President, I thank you for having invited the Palestine Liberation Organization to participate in the plenary session of the United Nations General Assembly. I am grateful to all those representatives of United Nations member states who contributed to the decision to introduce the question of Palestine as a separate item on the Agenda of this Assembly. That decision made possible the Assembly's resolution inviting us to address it on the question of Palestine.

This is a very important occasion. The question of Palestine is being reexamined by the United Nations, and we consider that step to be as much a victory for the world organization as it is for the cause of our people. It indicates anew that the United Nations of today is not the United Nations of the past, just as today's world is not yesterday's world. Today's United Nations represents 138 nations, a number that more clearly reflects the will of the international community. Thus today's United Nations is more capable of implementing the principles embodied in its Charter and in the Universal Declaration of Human Rights, as well as being more truly empowered to support causes of peace and justice.

Our people are now beginning to feel that change. Along with them, the peoples of Asia, Africa and Latin America also feel the change. As a result, the United Nations acquires greater esteem both in our people's view and in the view of other peoples. Our hope is thereby strengthened that the United Nations may contribute actively to the pursuit and triumph of the causes of peace, justice, freedom and independence. Our resolve to build a new world is fortified—a world free of colonialism, imperialism, neo-colonialism and racism in all its forms, including Zionism.

Victims of Oppression

Our world aspires to peace, justice, equality and freedom. It hopes that oppressed nations, at present bent under the weight of imperialism, may gain their freedom and their right to self-determination. . . .

Many peoples, including those of Zimbabwe, Namibia, South Africa and Palestine, among many others, are still victims of oppression and violence. Their areas of the world are gripped by armed struggles provoked by imperialism and racial discrimination. These, both merely forms of aggression and terror, are instances of oppressed peoples compelled by intolerable circumstances into a confrontation with such oppression. But wherever that confrontation occurs it is legitimate and just.

It is imperative that the international community should support these peoples in their struggles, in the furtherance of their rightful causes and in the attainment of their right to self-determination. . . .

In addressing the General Assembly today our people proclaims its faith in the future, unencumbered either by past tragedies or present limitations. If, as we discuss the present, we enlist the past in our service, we do so only to light up our journey into the future alongside other movements of national liberation. If we return now to the historical roots of our cause we do so because present at this very moment in our midst are those who, as they occupy our homes, as their cattle graze in our pastures, and as their hands pluck the fruit of our trees, claim at the same time that we are ghosts without an existence, without traditions or future. We speak of our roots also because until recently some people have regarded—and continue to regard—our problem as merely a problem of refugees. They have portrayed the Middle East question as little more than a border dispute between the Arab States and the Zionist entity. They have imagined that our people claim rights not rightfully their own and fight neither with logic nor legitimate motive, with a simple wish only to disturb the peace and to terrorize others. For there are amongst you—and here I refer to the United States of America and others like it—those who supply our enemy freely with planes and bombs and with every variety of murderous weapon. They take hostile positions against us, deliberately distorting the true essence of the problem. All this is done not only at our expense, but at the expense of the American people and its well-being, and of the friendship we continue to hope can be cemented between us and this great people, whose history of struggle for the sake of freedom and the unity of its territories we honour and salute.

The History of Palestine

In any event, in focusing our discussion of the question of Palestine upon historical roots, we do so because we believe that any question now exercising the world's concern must be viewed radically, in the true sense of that word, if a real solution is ever to be grasped. We propose this radical approach as an antidote to an approach to international issues that obscures historical origins behind ignorance, denial and a slavish obedience to the fait accompli.

The roots of the Palestinian question reach back into the closing years of the nineteenth century, in other words, to that period which we call the era of colonialism and settlement and the transition to the eve of imperialism. This was when the Zionist imperialist plan was born: its aim was the conquest of Palestine by European immigration, just as settlers colonized, and indeed raided, most of Africa. This is the period during which, pouring forth out of the West, colonialism spread into the furthest reaches of Africa, Asia, and Latin America, building colonies everywhere, cruelly exploiting, oppressing, plundering the peoples of those three continents. This period persists into the present. Marked evidence of its totally reprehensible presence can be readily perceived in the racism practised both in South Africa and in Palestine.

Just as colonialism and the settlers dignified their conquests, their plunder and limitless attacks upon the natives of Africa and elsewhere, with appeals to a "civilizing mission", so too did waves of Zionist immigrants disguise their purposes as they conquered Palestine. Just as colonialism used religion, colour, race and language to justify the people's exploitation and its cruel subjugation by terror and discrimination, so too were these methods employed as Palestine was usurped and its people hounded from their national homeland.

Just as colonialism used the wretched, the poor, the exploited as mere inert matter with which to build and to carry out settler colonialism, so too were destitute, oppressed European Jews employed on behalf of world imperialism and of the Zionist leadership. European Jews were transformed into the instruments of aggression; they became the elements of settler colonialism and racial discrimination.

Zionist ideology was utilized against our Palestinian people: the purpose was not only the establishment of Western-style settler colonialism but also the severing of Jews from their various homelands and subsequently their estrangement from their nations. Zionism is an ideology that is imperialistic, colonialist, racist; it is profoundly reactionary and discriminatory; it is united with anti-Semitism in its tenets and is the other side of the same coin. For when what is proposed is that adherents of the Jewish faith, regardless of their national residence, should neither owe allegiance to their homeland nor live on equal footing with its other, non-Jewish citizens—when that is proposed we hear anti-Semitism being proposed. When it is proposed that the only solution for the Jewish problem is that Jews must alienate themselves from communities or nations of which they have been a historical part, when it is proposed that Jews solve the Jewish problem by immigrating to and settling the land of another people by terrorism and force, this is exactly the same attitude as that of the anti-Semites to the Jews. . . .

The Jewish Invasion

The Jewish invasion of Palestine began in 1881. Before the first large wave of settlers started ariving, Palestine had a population of half a million, most of these Muslims or Christians, and about 10,000 Jews. Every sector of the population enjoyed the religious tolerance characteristics of our civilization.

Palestine was then a verdant land, inhabited by an Arab people in the course of building its life and enriching its indigenous culture.

Between 1882 and 1917 the Zionist movement settled approximately 50,000 European Jews in our homeland. To do that it resorted to trickery and deceit in order to plant them in our midst. Its success in getting Britain to issue the Balfour Declaration demonstrated the alliance between Zionism and colonialism. Furthermore, by promising to the Zionist movement what was not hers to give, Britain showed how oppressive the rule of colonialism was. As it was then constituted, the League of Nations abandoned our Arab people, and [U.S. President Woodrow] Wilson's pledges and promises came to nought. In the guise of a mandate, British colonialism was cruelly and directly imposed upon us. The mandate document issued by the League of Nations was to enable the Zionist invaders to consolidate their gains in our homeland.

In thirty years the Zionist movement succeeded, in collaboration with its colonialist ally, in settling more European Jews on the land, thus usurping the properties of Palestinian Arabs.

By 1947 the number of Jews had reached 600,000; they owned less than 6 per cent of Palestinian Arab land. The figure should be compared with the [Arab] population of Palestine, which at that time was 1,250,000.

As a result of the collusion between the mandatory power and the Zionist movement and with the support of the United States, this General Assembly early in its history approved a recommendation to partition our Palestinian homeland. This took place on November 30, 1947, in an atmosphere of questionable actions and strong pressure. The General Assembly partitioned what it had no right to divide—an indivisible homeland. When we rejected that decision, our position corresponded to that of the real mother who refused to permit Solomon to cut her child in two when the other woman claimed the child as hers. Furthermore, even though the partition resolution granted the colonialists settlers 54 per cent of the land of Palestine, their dissatisfaction with the decision prompted them to wage a war of terror against the civilian Arab population. They occupied 81 per cent of the total area of Palestine, uprooting a million Arabs. Thus, they occupied 524 Arab towns and villages, of which they destroyed 385, completely obliterating them in the process. Having done so, they built their own settlements and colonies on the ruins of our farms and our groves. The roots of the Palestine question lie here. Its causes do not stem from any conflict between two religions or two nationalisms. Nor is it a border conflict between neighbouring states. It is the cause of people deprived of its homeland, dispersed and uprooted, the majority of whom live in exile and in refugee camps. . . .

It pains our people greatly to witness the propagation of the myth that its homeland was a desert until it was made to bloom by the toil of foreign settlers, that it was a land without a people, and that the settler entity caused no harm to any human being. No, such lies must be exposed from this rostrum, for the world must know that Palestine was the cradle of the most ancient cultures and civilizations. Its Arab people were engaged in farming and building, spreading culture throughout the land for thousands of years, setting an example in the practice of religious tolerance and freedom of worship, acting as faithful guardians of the holy places of all religions. As a son of Jerusalem, I treasure for myself and my people beautiful memories and vivid images of the religious brotherhood that was the hallmark of our Holy City before it succumbed to catastrophe. Our people continued to pursue this enlightened policy until the establishment of the State of Israel and their dispersion. This did not deter our people from pursuing their humanitarian role on Palestinian soil. Nor will they permit their land to become a launching pad for aggression or a racist camp for the destruction of civilization, culture, progress and peace. Our people cannot but maintain the heritage of their ancestors in resisting the invaders, in assuming the privileged task of defending their native land, their Arab nationhood, their culture and civilization, and in safeguarding the cradle of the monotheistic religions. . . .

The Palestinian People

When the majority of the Palestinian people was uprooted from its homeland in 1948, the Palestinian struggle for self-determination continued in spite of efforts to destroy it. We tried every possible means to continue our political struggle to attain our national rights, but to no avail. Meanwhile we had to struggle for sheer existence. Even in exile we educated our children. This was all a part of trying to survive.

The Palestinian people have produced thousands of engineers, physicians, teachers and scientists who actively participated in the development of the Arab countries bordering on their usurped homeland. They have utilized their income to assist the young and aged amongst their people who could not leave the refugee camps. They have educated their younger brothers and sisters, have supported their parents and cared for their children. All along the Palestinian dreamt of return. Neither the Palestinian's allegiance to Palestine nor his determination to return waned; nothing could persuade him to relinquish his Palestinian identity or to forsake his homeland. The passage of time did not make him forget, as some hoped he would. When our people lost faith in the international community which persisted in ignoring its rights and when it became obvious that the Palestinians would not recoup one inch of Palestine through exclusively political means, our people had no choice but to resort to armed struggle. Into that struggle it poured its material and human resources and the flower of its youth. We bravely faced the most vicious acts of Israeli terrorism which were aimed at diverting our struggle and arresting it.

In the past ten years of our struggle, thousands of martyrs and twice as many wounded, maimed and imprisoned have been offered in sacrifice, all in an effort to resist the imminent threat of liquidation, to regain the right to self-determination and our right to return to our homeland. With the utmost dignity and the most admirable revolutionary spirit, our Palestinian people have not lost their spirit either in Israeli prisons and concentration camps or in the great prison of Israeli occupation. The people struggle for sheer existence and continue to strive to preserve the Arab character of their land. Thus they resist oppression, tyranny and terrorism in their grimmest forms.

It is through the armed revolution of our people that our political leadership and our national institutions finally crystallized and a national liberation movement, comprising all Palestinian factions, organizations and capabilities, materialized in the Palestine Liberation Organization.

The Palestine Liberation Organization

Through our militant Palestine national liberation movement our people's struggle has matured and grown enough to accommodate political and social struggle in addition to armed struggle. The Palestine Liberation Organization has been a major factor in creating a new Palestinian individual, qualified to shape the future of our Palestine, not merely content with mobilizing the Palestinians for the challenges of the present.

The Palestine Liberation Organization can be proud of having a large number of cultural and educational activities, even while engaged in armed struggle, and at a time when it faced the increasingly vicious blows of Zionist terrorism. We have established institutes for scientific research, agricultural development and social welfare, as well as centres for the revival of our cultural heritage and the preservation of our folklore. Many Palestinian poets, artists and writers have enriched Arab culture in particular, and world culture generally. Their profoundly humane works have won the admiration of all those familiar with them. In contrast to that, our enemy has been systematically destroying our culture and disseminating racist, colonialist ideologies; in short, everything that impedes progress, justice, democracy and peace.

The Palestine Liberation Organization has earned its legitimacy because of the sacrifice inherent in its pioneering role, and also because of its dedicated leadership of the struggle. It has also been granted this legitimacy by the Palestinian masses, which in harmony with it have chosen it to lead the struggle according to its directives. The Palestine Liberation Organization has also gained its legitimacy by representing every faction, union or group as well as every Palestinian talent, either in the National Council or in people's institutions. This legitimacy was further strengthened by the support of the entire Arab nation which supports it, and further consecrated during the last Arab Summit Conference, which affirmed the right of the Palestine Liberation Organization, in its capacity as the sole representative of the Palestinian people, to establish an independent national authority on all liberated Palestinian territory. . . .

The Palestine Liberation Organization represents the Palestinian people. Because of this, the Palestine Liberation Organization expresses the wishes and hopes of its people. Because of this, too, it brings these very wishes and hopes before you, urging you not to shirk a momentous historic responsibility towards our just cause. . . .

I am a rebel and freedom is my cause, I know well that many of you present here today once stood in exactly the same position of resistance as I now occupy and from which I must fight. You once had to convert dreams into reality by your struggle. Therefore you must now share my dream. I think this is exactly why I can ask you now to help, as together we bring out our dream into a bright reality, our common dream for a peaceful future in Palestine's sacred land. . . .

A Generous Offer

In my capacity as Chairman of the Palestine Liberation Organization and commander of the Palestinian revolution I proclaim before you that when we speak of our common hopes for the Palestine of tomorrow we include in our perspective all Jews now living in Palestine who choose to live with us there in peace and without discrimination.

In my capacity as commander of the forces of the Palestine Liberation Organization I call upon Jews to turn away one by one from the illusory promises made to them by Zionist ideology and Israeli leadership. They are offering Jews perpetual bloodshed, endless war and continuous thralldom.

We invite them to emerge into a more open realm of free choice, far from their present leadership's efforts to implant in them a Masada complex [to die rather than surrender] and make it their destiny.

We offer them the most generous solution—that we should live together in a framework of just peace in our democratic Palestine.

In my formal capacity as Chairman of the Palestine Liberation Organization I announce here that we do not wish one drop of either Jewish or Arab blood to be shed; neither do we delight in the continuation of killings for a single moment, once a just peace, based on our people's rights, hopes, and aspirations has been finally established.

In my capacity as Chairman of the Palestine Liberation Organization and commander of the Palestinian revolution I appeal to you to accompany our people in its struggle to attain its right to self-determination. This right is consecrated in the United Nations Charter and has been repeatedly confirmed in resolutions adopted by this august body since the drafting of the Charter. I appeal to you, further, to aid our people's return to its homeland from an involuntary exile imposed upon it by force of arms, by tyranny, by oppression, so that we may regain our property, our land, and thereafter live in our national homeland, free and sovereign, enjoying all the privileges of nationhood.

I appeal to you to enable our people to set up their national authority and establish their national entity in their own land.

Only then will our people be able to contribute all their energies and resources to the field of civilization and human creativity. Only then will they be able to protect their beloved Jerusalem and make it, as they have done for so many centuries, the shrine of all religions, free from all terrorism and coercion.

Today I have come bearing an olive branch and a freedom-fighter's gun. Do not let the olive branch fall from my hand. Do not let the olive branch fall from my hand. Do not let the olive branch fall from my hand.

War flares up in Palestine, and yet it is in Palestine that peace will be born.

Why We Need a Jewish State

Golda Meir

Golda Meir was born in the Soviet Union in 1898. Eight years later her family moved to Milwaukee. In 1921 she moved to Palestine and settled in Kibbutz Merhaviah. She originally worked for the Women's Labor Council, but by circumstance she became a major figure in Israeli politics after June 29, 1946, when the British arrested almost all the members of the political elite, which operated within the Jewish Agency (the Jewish governing body in Palestine). The Jewish leadership was opposed to the continued British presence in the region and endorsed guerrilla attacks on the British police forces. With little opposition, Meir was chosen to head the new Jewish Agency. She had previously opposed the partitioning of Palestine, but in response to the Holocaust, she became a fierce advocate of carving out a Jewish State. Her opinions earned her respect, and Meir would become Israel's fourth prime minister in 1969.

This speech was given in December 1946 at the Twenty-second Zionist Congress in Basle, Switzerland. The Zionist congresses were started in 1897 by Theodore Herzl to unite all Zionists around the world under one movement. The congress in 1946 was the first to convene following the end of World War II. In it, Meir, as head of the Jewish Agency, rails against the British Government for its false promises for greater autonomy for Jews in Palestine and its treatment of Jews immigrating to Palestine. She tells a grim story of the ship *Exodus* bringing European Jews to Zion. The British mandate contained

strict immigration limits on Jews entering the area, which
were strongly opposed by Meir and the Jewish Agency
who saw the restrictions as Britain's way of maintaining
imperial control within the Middle East. The British authorities stopped the *Exodus* just off Haifa intending to
send the immigrants back to Europe. Many on board
jumped into the sea and tried to swim to shore. The
British fired on some and many others drowned in their
attempt to reach their homeland.

Meir also dismisses the supposed schism between
Zionist and non-Zionist Jews, and any animosity that
might exist between them. She claims there is only one
Jewish identity and that rests with the Jewish homeland in
Palestine. She often refers to "Palestinians" in her speech,
meaning Jews living in Palestine, not Arab Palestinians.
Meir was a major power broker in the debate and her
words influenced such British politicians as Winston
Churchill, who eventually argued in the following years
that Britain relinquish control of the region. The eventual
removal of British forces led to the Israeli War of Independence and the establishment of the Jewish State.

The present Labor government of Great Britain refuses
to implement resolutions passed and promises made
at conventions of the Labor Party over the past thirty
years. These British politicians see no need to honor pledges
made not only to us, but to millions of British workers and
soldiers and to the British people. Now, after the war, we witness deeds committed in Palestine unusual even in our history, replete as it is with cruel decrees. Instead of freedom—
suppression; instead of preparation for a Jewish state in
Palestine—the expulsion of Jews from the country.

We see how Jews are killed near the shore, on the border
of Palestine, by British soldiers, men who had been mobilized
not for war with Jewish immigrants, but sent by their nation
to fight Hitler and not the Jews. This government, instead of
helping us to lay the foundation for a Jewish state and Jewish independence in Palestine, is trying to deprive us of what

little independence, what little administrative authority we have laboriously achieved by our own energy.

A Jewish State

Why are we now pressing our demand for a Jewish state? When did it become clear to us that we must have absolute control over our lives and immigration, that this must be in the hands of Jews not as a distant aim, but as a desperate, immediate need? We understood this necessity the moment that we, 600,000 Jews in Palestine, despite all that we had created in the country and endured during the long years of war, stood powerless to rescue hundreds and thousands of Jews, perhaps millions, from certain death. The only obstacle between our readiness to rescue the Jews of Europe and the terrible certainty that death awaited them at Hitler's hands, the only thing that blocked their way from death to life, was a political regulation laid down by strangers—the White Paper![1] The British government stood between us and millions of Jews lost in Europe. Various excuses were found to explain to us why it was impossible to rescue Jews: There was "a lack of ships" to bring Jews ("Was there not a war going on and was it not necessary to transport troops?"). We heard many replies to the question of why Jewish children could not be brought to Palestine. But ships were found to transport Jews from Palestine far away to Mauritius—for that there was no hindrance. In the moments when the *Struma* sank on our shores, when hundreds of Jews were lost practically within our very sight, and we the Jewish Yishuv, who felt ourselves during the war to be the nerve center of European Jewry in all its torments, could be of no help because this White Paper stood as an iron wall between us and the victims of Hitler, when Palestine youth were straining to reach the Jews in the ghettos, to be with them, to unite them and prepare them to revolt, and we could not do this except with the consent of others, when our helplessness was so tragically revealed to us, then the argument among us about

1. Issued by the British government in 1939, the White Paper called for constraints on Jewish immigration to Palestine.

the goals of Zionism ceased. Zionism, redemption, and rescue coalesced into one concept; if there are no Jews, there is no redemption; if there is to be redemption, a free Jewish people, Jews must first be rescued from death and destruction and brought to Palestine.

During the war years it became evident to us that no foreign government would bring Jews to Palestine, that no government would feel the agony as we feel it, and that no government would long to save Jews and rescue Jewish lives as we long to do. It is therefore impossible for us to go on in this manner and acquiesce in the fact that our desire to rescue, to build, and to bring Jews to Palestine should be entirely dependent on outsiders. And it became obvious to us that a state was a necessity for us not as a last resort but as an immediate instrument for the rescue of Jews and the upbuilding of Palestine. We must become the masters of our undertaking. Only then will we be able to accomplish whatever is vital to the life of the Jewish people without begging the indulgence of others and as we deem fit.

I will not dwell at length over what we went through in Palestine during the war years. We wanted with all our heart to participate in the war. We claimed that the fight concerned us first and foremost, for it was on us that it was first declared. As long as the war was only against the Jews, we stood alone, without allies; however, once the war embraced the entire world and we wanted to join and fight with all our strength, a long and dolorous chapter commenced. Finally, our youth breached the wall and won the right to go to the front as a Jewish unit. Imagine for yourselves what we went through before permission was granted for a few dozens of our comrades to be dropped as parachutists behind the lines in the occupied countries, there to contact the Jews, bring tidings of Palestine, encourage them, and assist them to rebel against the conquerors; consider what we in Palestine felt when we were forced to seek all manner of stratagems to provide what little help we could to Jews in the charnelhouse of Eastern Europe!

During the war we were also afforded an insight into the nature of a government which is indifferent to the interests of the people it governs. The economic regime in Palestine during the war was such as to indicate that the government cared nothing for the welfare of the Palestine economy or whether it emerged from the war strong and healthy and able to compete with other countries. We often suspected—and let us not be accused of exaggerating!—that the government's economic system was designed so that Palestine should not be on a competitive footing.

At every turn—ranging from the crucial task of saving Jewish lives to lesser matters such as maintaining a healthy economy so that we might be able to absorb a large immigration—it became clear to us daily that the only way of fulfilling Zionism in the present situation was a Jewish state. The fact that the Zionist movement and the Jewish people found the courage during the war years to declare openly that in Jewry's present situation there was only one solution to the Jewish question—the establishment of a Jewish state—was one of the few rays of light in the dark days of war; and not only for us and American Jewry, but—more important—for Jews in the ghettos and forests.

Recent Events

We had truly hoped that a better world would emerge when the war was over, and that then the rights of the Jewish people would be recognized. This did not happen. Instead, the British government began to make declarations "proving" that a schism existed among Jews. [British foreign minister Ernest] Bevin set out to divide the Jews into Zionists and non-Zionists, extremists and nonextremists. Thereafter he started dividing the Jews into those who wished to immigrate to Palestine and those who had no such wish. When the British government and the Palestine government proceeded to explain the outrageous actions of June 29 [when the members of the Jewish Agency were arrested], against the elected representatives of the Jewish community of Palestine, they announced that everything which took place that day was actually aimed against the extremists, whereas no harm would befall decent people. On that Saturday morning, at seven thirty, we heard on the radio from the high commissioner that the entire Yishuv (the Jewish community) could sit back

quietly: Moderate and decent Jews would not be harmed. Action was being taken only against a few extremist and harmful individuals of the Jewish Agency, the National Executive,
the Executive Committee of the Histadrut Workers' Federation, and some thirty settlements throughout the country.
Other than these "handfuls," the entire Yishuv were decent
people who had nothing to fear; no one would harm them.

Once the British government embarked on this path, the
Yishuv was faced with two options: either to tell Bevin and
his colleagues in the Cabinet: "You were right, there is such
a division, and by following this path you may possibly accomplish what you want," or to speak decisively: "The Jewish people, the Yishuv, the Zionist movement are one in their
aims."

Our Zionist friends living afar may possibly allow themselves to exaggerate the strength of the Yishuv in Palestine;
we do not, of course, wish to be belittled, but we must be-
ware of exaggerating the extent of our strength. We, the
Palestinians, unfortunately cannot permit ourselves the luxury of fantasy. We must calculate our strength with detachment. Nevertheless, we decided to muster all our capacity
and do two things simultaneously: first, to continue our
building in Palestine without pause; second, to convince England that the Yishuv would fight any attempt to submit the
issue of our settlement in Palestine to the will of another
people who would not permit us to bring Jews into Palestine
in accordance with the need of the Jews and the absorption
capacity of the country. We would accept no decree stifling
our growth.

When the Jewish survivors in the DP [displaced persons]
camps [in Europe at the end of World War II] were asked
whether they wished to go to America, to Australia, or to
other countries, it might well have been natural for these tortured souls, remnants not only of the Jewish people but of
families, communities, and entire countries, to have instantly
grasped such offers with open arms. Yet these Jews—in DP
camp after camp—replied as one: "Let there be an end to our
worldwide wandering. We have but one home—Palestine!"

I do not know if the Zionist world and the Jewish world
are aware of what it meant to us that these few Jews have

survived not only for themselves, but for us as well. The primary thing is that they have survived, and the second—that having survived, they were aware of what the present time required of them and of what Zionism means today in the life of the Jews! That is a miracle.

What Immigrants to Zion Face

And we have witnessed another miracle—the reaction of our sabras, boys and girls born in Palestine, who knew nothing of the Diaspora and had very rarely seen Diaspora Jews [those living outside Israel] with the exception of those who had come to Palestine—a youth who had no memory of the Jewish *stetl* with its tribulations, traditions, and marvelous Jewish life. Our sabras, growing up in Palestine erect and confident, were ready to sacrifice themselves without fear for European Jewry. From time to time we used to ask ourselves anxiously: What is to bind these children of ours to the Jewish people, the major portion of whom is still abroad? The time came when the sabras themselves gave the answer. These young people are strangers to casuistry and abstract precepts; they are plain and pure as the sun of Palestine. For them, matters are simple, clear, and uncomplicated. When the catastrophe descended upon the Jews of the world, and Jews began coming to Palestine in "illegal" ships, as they still do, we saw these children of ours go down to the seas and at risk to their lives—this is no rhetoric, but literally so—ford the waves to reach the boats and bear these Jews ashore on their shoulders. This, too, is no rhetoric, no flowery speech, but the literal truth: sixteen- and eighteen-year-old Palestinian girls and boys carried the survivors on their backs. From the mouths of Jews borne on their shoulders I have heard that they shed tears for the first time, after all they had been through in Europe for seven years, on seeing a Palestinian youth bearing grown men and women to the soil of the homeland. We have been blessed in this youth, which makes no account of the degree of danger or self-sacrifice, but simply, with a sure dedication, sets out to offer its life not in behalf of its own particular kibbutz, or of the Yishuv in Palestine in general, but for the sake of every Jewish child or old man seeking entry.

Since the British government has terminated immigration by certificate, the path leading Jews to Palestine will have to be independent of the British government's permits; if Jews are not given certificates, they will immigrate to Palestine without permits, and they so immigrate! Theirs is no easy path. However, Jews are prepared to embark in the "illegal" ships despite their knowledge that immigration to Palestine means that they will arrive off the coast of Haifa, where they will be met by troops who will shower blows and gas bombs on them; some of them will be killed, and those killed will not even be brought to Jewish burial. If they are lucky, they will have the privilege of being led to a fresh detention camp in Cyprus! Notwithstanding all this, Jews set out—young and old—and children are born in the terrible boats. As I have said before, this is one miracle. The other miracle is that the youth of Palestine is doing its utmost in the struggle on their behalf.

Free Jewish immigration into Palestine does not depend on the British government, but on the Jews themselves and on Zionists throughout the world. Our chief demand at present concerns immigration—that it should increase, that ever more ships should come, that many thousands of survivors should come to Palestine every month. And while the British government is engaged in debating for a year about immigration certificates for 100,000 Jews, we must transform this matter in short order into an accomplished fact. We must transport the 100,000 Jews to Palestine in our own ships, and bring them in with our own means.

Britain's Attempts to Cripple Jewish Resolve

The twenty-ninth of June, when the British government arrested the leaders of the Yishuv, was a turning point in Palestine. In this action the government overreached itself. It is not true, that searches for arms commenced on the twenty-ninth of June or that this was the government's response to various Haganah acts performed in Palestine before that date. Palestinians and non-Palestinians alike remember Ramat Hakovesh and Hulda, when the British started searching for arms among us. At Ramat Hakovesh the British came to search for arms shortly after the disturbances in which members of this settlement fell almost daily. On the twenty-ninth of June the government set out to break the spirit and backbone of the Yishuv in Palestine by one concentrated blow. That day the government fell upon us; the troops it sent against us assaulted the Jewish Agency building, occupied it, and held it for a week; that day, on a Saturday morning, the members of the Executive and of the National Council were led off as prisoners; in one morning the British occupied dozens of settlements and attempted forcibly to confiscate the arms which the government well knew were essential for our defense. In one day they filled detention camps with close to 4,000 Jewish prisoners. In doing all this, the government sought to break the fighting spirit of the Yishuv in Palestine. By its actions, the government wished to smash whatever independence the Jews had acquired in Palestine. In taking the Agency building, it proposed to manifest to all that the Jews were deluding themselves in believing that they were independent and could elect leaders of their own choice.

It was not long before the government realized its ignominious defeat. Though there might have been differences of opinion about tactics in the Yishuv, sound Jewish political sense dictated that when the hand of strangers was raised against our independence, Jews would draw tightly together. Above all, these blows strengthened our determination to demand that full measure of political independence which can be attained only through the establishment of a Jewish state.

Britain Should Pull Out of Palestine

Winston Churchill

Winston Churchill was a major player in the establishment of a Jewish state. He first became involved in the region as colonial secretary of Great Britain from 1921 to 1922. He issued the first official White Paper that supported a Jewish State in certain parts of Palestine but not at the expense of subordinating the Arab population, language, or culture. In 1944, as prime minister of Britain, he proposed the partitioning of Palestine into two states, one Arab and the other Jewish. This measure was approved by the United Nations General Assembly in 1947 and became known as the Partition Plan. The Jews accepted the plan. The Arabs rejected it.

While no longer prime minister, Churchill was still a powerful force in British politics when he gave the following speech in January 1947. Churchill was addressing the British House of Commons and his words are highly critical of the British government for its treatment of Jews in Palestine and its failure to ensure stability in the region. He refers to several broken promises—promises made to the Jews in Palestine for greater autonomy. Churchill makes the point that a long-term supervision of the region is no longer economically feasible. He refers to attacks upon British soldiers and personnel by both Arabs and Jews as he makes his (not necessarily altruistic) case for why Great Britain should withdraw permanently from the Middle East. In 1948, the British Government finally abandoned its claims to Palestine. Churchill's words were compelling, and struggling with its own eco-

---

Winston Churchill, address to the House of Commons, January 31, 1947.

nomic reconstruction after World War II, England decided to abandon its major interests in Palestine. In this power vacuum, Jewish leaders declared Israeli statehood.

The House has listened to two speeches from opposite sides of the Chamber, both of which have been characterised by a great deal of knowledge and thought, and distinguished if I may say so, by grace of delivery. Both these Members have evidently acquainted themselves closely with the problems of maintaining law and order in Palestine. We should all agree with my hon. and gallant Friend the Member for Macclesfield [Air-Commodore Harvey] in the tribute which he paid, and which other speakers have also paid, to the behaviour and restraint which our troops have observed. None of us underestimates the prolonged trial, not only physical but moral, to which they have been subjected by this series of detestable outrages.

A Struggle That Has Achieved Nothing

The hon. Member for Grimsby [Mr. Younger] said that it was impossible for us to imitate the mass extermination methods of the Germans. There, again, we would all be in agreement. The idea that general reprisals upon the civil population and vicarious examples would be consonant with our whole outlook upon the world and with our name, reputation and principles, is, of course, one which should never be accepted in any way. We have, therefore, very great difficulties in conducting squalid warfare with terrorists. That is why I would venture to submit to the House that every effort should be made to avoid getting into warfare with terrorists; and if a warfare with terrorists has broken out, every effort should be made—I exclude no reasonable proposal—to bring it to an end.

It is quite certain that what is going on now in Palestine is doing us a great deal of harm in every way. Whatever view is taken by the partisans of the Jews or the partisans of the Arabs it is doing us harm in our reputation all over the world.

I deplore very much this struggle that we have got into. I do not think we ought to have got into it. I think it could have been avoided. It could have been avoided if promises had not been made by hon. Members opposite at the Election, on a very wide scale, and if those promises had not been woefully disappointed. I must say that. All my hon. Friends on this side of the House do not agree with the views which I have held for so many years about the Zionist cause. But promises were made far beyond those to which responsible Governments should have committed themselves. What has been the performance? The performance has been a vacuum, a gaping void, a senseless, dumb abyss—nothing. . . .

No Recompense for Our Efforts

This is a lamentable situation. However we may differ, it is one of the most unhappy, unpleasant situations into which we have got, even in these troublous years. Here, we are expending hard-earned money at an enormous rate in Palestine. Everyone knows what our financial difficulties are—how heavy the

weight of taxation. We are spending a vast sum of money on this business. For 18 months we have been pouring out our wealth on this unhappy, unfortunate and discreditable business. Then there is the manpower of at least 100,000 men in Palestine, who might well be at home strengthening our defeated industry. What are they doing there? What good are we getting out of it?

We are told that there are a handful of terrorists on one side and 100,000 British troops on the other. How much does it cost? No doubt it is £300 a year

Winston Churchill

per soldier in Palestine. That is apart from what I call a slice of the overheads, which is enormous, of the War Office and other Services. That is £30 million a year. It may be much more—between £30 million and £40 million a year—which is being poured out and which would do much to help to find employment in these islands, or could be allowed to return to fructify in the pockets of the people—to use a phrase which has dropped out of discussion now, but which was much in vogue at one time in Liberal circles, together with all sorts of antiquated ideas about the laws of supply and demand by people like Adam Smith, John Stuart Mill, and other worthies of that kind. One hundred thousand men is a very definite proportion of our Army for one and a half years. How much longer are they to stay there? And stay for what? In order that on a threat to kill hostages we show ourselves unable to execute a sentence duly pronounced by a competent tribunal. It is not good enough. I never saw anything less recompensive for the efforts now employed than what is going on in Palestine.

Flawed Arguments for Remaining

Then we are told, "Oh, well, we must stay there because we have evacuated Egypt, and we need a place for strategic purposes in order to guard the [Suez] Canal". I should have thought that was a very wrong idea. At any rate, you have an easement in this respect, because the negotiations already clumsily begun with Egypt have ended in a reversion, as the Prime Minister promised, to the 1936 Treaty, which has another 10 years to run. Let us then stay in the Canal Zone and have no further interest in the strategic aspects of Palestine. At any rate, there is that argument, but I have never thought that we had a strategic interest there. I have always believed that in other ways we should maintain our interests. But then one may say, "We have to stay there because of our faith and honour". Good gracious, sir, we cannot say that. We have broken our pledges to the Jews. We have not fulfilled the promise made at the Election, and, having found ourselves incapable of carrying out our policy, we have no right to say, "Oh, we have to stay there from motives of honour". Then others say, "You must stay, because, if you go, Jew and Arab will be at each other's throats". It is said there will be a civil war. I think it is very likely indeed, but is that a reason why

we should stay? We do not propose to stay in India, even if
a civil war of a gigantic character were to follow our departure. No, that is all brushed aside. We are not going to allow
such things to make us stay. We are told to leave the Indians
to settle their own affairs by getting a verdict from a body
which is unrepresentative and then march out. In Palestine
we are told we cannot go, because it would lead to a terrible
quarrel between Jews and Arabs and there would be civil war
as to who would have the land.

I do not feel myself at all convinced by such arguments.
If it be the case, first, that there is no British interest—which
I declare with a long experience that there is not—then the
responsibility for stopping a civil war in Palestine between
Jew and Arab ought to be borne by the United Nations, and
not by this poor overburdened and heavily injured country. I
think it is too much to allow this heavy burden to be put on
our shoulders costing £30 million a year and keeping
100,000 men from their homes. I see absolutely no reason
why we should undergo all this pain, toil, injury and suffering because of this suggested advantage.

Israel Must Adhere to International Law

Dwight D. Eisenhower

In the early 1950s, Israel was suffering from increased attacks from the fedayeen—Palestinians trained and supported by Egypt. Israeli attempts to repel the attacks, which mainly came from the Gaza region, were unsuccessful. In 1956, Egypt nationalized the Suez Canal and other properties belonging to Great Britain and France and openly supported anti-French rebels in North Africa. Intent on stopping the support for Palestinian guerrillas, Israel joined forces with Britain and France and invaded Egypt, launching the Sinai War. The combined forces drove deep into Egyptian territory before a cease-fire was called. Once victory was obtained, the Anglo-French forces quickly withdrew from Egypt, leaving Israel with control of the Suez Canal and the Sinai Peninsula.

Although the United Nations believed Egypt had learned its lesson, Israel was hesitant to pull out of the territory it gained in the war, claiming the area was necessary to guarantee Israeli safety from future attacks. American president Dwight D. Eisenhower disagreed. In a speech before the United Nations, he strongly urges Israel to respect UN policies that call for removal of Israeli forces from Egyptian territory. He had previously spoken to the United Nations on this topic just four months earlier, producing few changes. Though Eisenhower was best known as a great general, he states that the use of force cannot be used as a means of settling international differences. What becomes clear in his speech is Eisenhower's support for the United Nations and his contempt for the

Dwight D. Eisenhower, address to the United Nations, February 20, 1957.

Soviet Union, which had been supplying weapons to Egypt throughout the conflict. Eisenhower's condemnation of the Soviet support for terrorists was in part an attempt to maintain moral superiority over the Soviet Union in these early days of the Cold War.

In 1957, Israel finally bowed to pressure from Eisenhower and withdrew from the occupied territory. Furthermore, it allowed the United Nations Emergency Force (UNEF) to patrol the armistice line between Israel and Egypt.

I come to you again to talk about the situation in the Middle East. The future of the United Nations and peace in the Middle East may be at stake.

In the 4 months since I talked to you about the crisis in that area, the United Nations has made considerable progress in resolving some of the difficult problems. We are now, however, faced with a fateful moment as the result of the failure of Israel to withdraw its forces behind the armistice lines; as contemplated by the United Nations resolutions on this subject.

I have already today met with leaders of both parties from the Senate and the House of Representatives. We had a very useful exchange of views. It was the general feeling of that meeting that I should lay the situation before the American people.

Now, before talking about the specific issues involved, I want to make clear that these issues are not something remote and abstract but involve matters vitally touching upon the future of each one of us.

The Middle East is a land bridge between the Eurasian and African continents. Millions of tons of commerce are transmitted through it annually. Its own products, especially petroleum, are essential to Europe and the Western World.

The United States has no ambitions or desires in this region. It hopes only that each country there may maintain its independence and live peacefully within itself and with its neighbors and, by peaceful cooperation with others, develop its own spiritual and material resources. But that much is vital to the peace and well-being of us all. This is our concern today.

So tonight I report to you on the matters in controversy and on what I believe the position of the United States must be.

Seeking Peace

When I talked to you last October, I pointed out that the United States fully realized that military action against Egypt resulted from grave and repeated provocations. But I said also that the use of military force to solve international disputes could not be reconciled with the principles and purposes of the United Nations. I added that our country could not believe that resort to force and war would for long serve the permanent interests of the attacking nations, which were Britain, France, and Israel.

So I pledged that the United States would seek through the United Nations to end the conflict. We would strive to bring about a recall of the forces of invasion and then make a renewed and earnest effort through that organization to secure justice, under international law, for all the parties concerned.

Since that time much has been achieved and many of the dangers implicit in the situation have been avoided. The Governments of Britain and France have withdrawn their forces from Egypt. Thereby they showed respect for the opinions of mankind as expressed almost unanimously by the 80 nation members of the United Nations General Assembly.

I want to pay tribute to the wisdom of this action of our friends and allies. They made an immense contribution to world order. Also they put the other nations of the world under a heavy obligation to see to it that these two nations do not suffer by reason of their compliance with the United Nations resolutions. This has special application, I think, to their treaty rights to passage through the Suez Canal, which had been made an international waterway for all by the treaty of 1888.

The Prime Minister of Israel, in answer to a personal communication, assured me early in November that Israel

would willingly withdraw its forces if and when there should
be created a United Nations force to move into the Suez
Canal area. This force was, in fact, created and has moved
into the canal area.

Subsequently, Israeli forces were withdrawn from much
of the territory of Egypt which they had occupied. However,
Israeli forces still remain outside the armistice lines. They are
at the mouth of the Gulf of Aqaba, which is about 100 miles
from the nearest Israeli territory. They are also in the Gaza
Strip, which, by the Armistice Agreement, was to be occupied
by Egypt. These facts create the present crisis.

Efforts to Bring About Israeli Withdrawal

We are approaching a fateful moment when either we must
recognize that the United Nations is unable to restore peace
in this area or the United Nations must renew with increased
vigor its efforts to bring about Israeli withdrawal.

Repeated, but, so far, unsuccessful, efforts have been
made to bring about a voluntary withdrawal by Israel. These
efforts have been made both by the United Nations and by
the United States and other member states.

Equally serious efforts have been made to bring about
conditions designed to assure that, if Israel will withdraw in
response to the repeated requests of the United Nations,
there will then be achieved a greater security and tranquillity
for that nation. This means that the United Nations would
assert a determination to see that in the Middle East there
will be a greater degree of justice and compliance with international law than was the case prior to the events of last October–November.

A United Nations Emergency Force, with Egypt's consent, entered that nation's territory in order to help maintain
the cease-fire which the United Nations called for on November 2. The Secretary-General, who ably and devotedly
serves the United Nations, has recommended a number of
measures which might be taken by the United Nations and
by its Emergency Force to assure for the future the avoidance
by either side of belligerent acts.

The United Nations General Assembly on February 2 by an overwhelming vote adopted a pertinent resolution. It was to the effect that, after full withdrawal of Israel from the Gulf of Aqaba and Gaza areas, the United Nations Emergency Force should be placed on the Egyptian-Israeli armistice lines to assure the scrupulous maintenance of the Armistice Agreement. Also the United Nations General Assembly called for the implementation of other measures proposed by the Secretary-General. These other measures embraced the use of the United Nations Emergency Force at the mouth of the Gulf of Aqaba, so as to assure nonbelligerency in this area.

The United States was a cosponsor of this United Nations resolution. Thus the United States sought to assure that Israel would, for the future, enjoy its rights under the armistice and under international law.

In view of the valued friendly relations which the United States has always had with the State of Israel, I wrote to Prime Minister BenGurion on February 3. I recalled his statement to me of November 8 to the effect that the Israeli forces would be withdrawn under certain conditions, and I urged that, in view of the General Assembly resolutions of February 2, Israel should complete that withdrawal.

However, the Prime Minister, in his reply, took the position that Israel would not evacuate its military forces from the Gaza Strip unless Israel retained the civil administration and police. This would be in contradiction to the Armistice Agreement. Also, the reply said that Israel would not withdraw from the Straits of Aqaba unless freedom of passage through the straits was assured.

It was a matter of keen disappointment to us that the Government of Israel, despite the United Nations action, still felt unwilling to withdraw.

Statement of U.S. Policy

However, in a further effort to meet the views of Israel in these respects, Secretary of State Dulles, at my direction, gave to the Government of Israel on February 11 a statement of United States policy. This has now been made public. It pointed out that neither the United States nor the United Nations had authority to impose upon the parties a substantial modification of the Armistice Agreement which was freely signed by both Israel and Egypt. Nevertheless, the statement said, the United States as a member of the United Nations would seek such disposition of the United Nations Emergency Force as would assure that the Gaza Strip could no longer be used as a source of armed infiltration and reprisals.

The Secretary of State orally informed the Israeli Ambassador that the United States would be glad to urge and support, also, some participation by the United Nations, with the approval of Egypt, in the administration of the Gaza Strip. The principal population of the strip consists of about 200,000 Arab refugees, who exist largely as a charge upon the benevolence of the United Nations and its members.

With reference to the passage into and through the Gulf of Aqaba, we expressed the conviction that the gulf constitutes international waters and that no nation has the right to prevent free and innocent passage in the gulf. We announced that the United States was prepared to exercise this right itself and to join with others to secure general recognition of this right.

The Government of Israel has not yet accepted, as adequate insurance of its own safety after withdrawal, the far-reaching United Nations resolution of February 2, plus the important declaration of United States policy made by our Secretary of State on February 11.

Israel seeks something more. It insists on firm guaranties as a condition to withdrawing its forces of invasion.

This raises a basic question of principle. Should a nation which attacks and occupies foreign territory in the face of United Nations disapproval be allowed to impose conditions on its own withdrawal?

If we agree that armed attack can properly achieve the purposes of the assailant, then I fear we will have turned back the clock of international order. We will, in effect, have countenanced the use of force as a means of settling international differences and through this gaining national advantages.

I do not, myself, see how this could be reconciled with the charter of the United Nations. The basic pledge of all the members of the United Nations is that they will settle their international disputes by peaceful means and will not use force against the territorial integrity of another state.

If the United Nations once admits that international disputes can be settled by using force, then we will have destroyed the very foundation of the organization and our best hope of establishing a world order. That would be a disaster for us all.

I would, I feel, be untrue to the standards of the high office to which you have chosen me if I were to lend the influence of the United States to the proposition that a nation which invades another should be permitted to exact conditions for withdrawal.

Justice and International Law

Of course, we and all the members of the United Nations ought to support justice and conformity with international law. The first article of the charter states the purpose of the United Nations to be "the suppression of acts of aggression or other breaches of the peace, and to bring about by peaceful means, and in conformity with . . . justice and international law, adjustment or settlement of international disputes." But it is to be observed that conformity with justice and international law are to be brought about "by peaceful means."

We cannot consider that the armed invasion and occupation of another country are "peaceful means" or proper means to achieve justice and conformity with international law.

We do, however, believe that upon the suppression of the present act of aggression and breach of the peace there should be greater effort by the United Nations and its members to secure justice and conformity with international law. Peace and justice are two sides of the same coin.

Perhaps the world community has been at fault in not having paid enough attention to this basic truth. The United States, for its part, will vigorously seek solutions of the problems of the area in accordance with justice and international law. And we shall in this great effort seek the association of other like-minded nations which realize, as we do, that peace and justice are in the long run inseparable.

But the United Nations faces immediately the problem of

what to do next. If it does nothing, if it accepts the ignoring of its repeated resolutions calling for the withdrawal of invading forces, then it will have admitted failure. That failure would be a blow to the authority and influence of the United Nations in the world and to the hopes which humanity placed in the United Nations as the means of achieving peace with justice.

I do not believe that Israel's default should be ignored because the United Nations has not been able effectively to carry out its resolutions condemning the Soviet Union for its armed suppression of the people of Hungary. Perhaps this is a case where the proverb applies that two wrongs do not make a right.

No one deplores more than I the fact that the Soviet Union ignores the resolutions of the United Nations. Also no nation is more vigorous than is the United States in seeking to exert moral pressure against the Soviet Union, which by reason of its size and power, and by reason of its veto in the Security Council, is relatively impervious to other types of sanction.

The United States and other free nations are making clear by every means at their command the evil of Soviet conduct in Hungary. It would indeed be a sad day if the United States ever felt that it had to subject Israel to the same type of moral pressure as is being applied to the Soviet Union.

There can, of course, be no equating of a nation like Israel with that of the Soviet Union. The people of Israel, like those of the United States, are imbued with a religious faith and a sense of moral values. We are entitled to expect, and do expect, from such peoples of the free world a contribution to world order which unhappily we cannot expect from a nation controlled by atheistic despots.

It has been suggested that United Nations actions against Israel should not be pressed because Egypt has in the past violated the Armistice Agreement and international law. It is true that both Egypt and Israel, prior to last October, engaged in reprisals in violation of the Armistice Agreements. Egypt ignored the United Nations in exercising belligerent rights in relation to Israeli shipping in the Suez Canal and in the Gulf of Aqaba. However, such violations constitute no justification for the armed invasion of Egypt by Israel which the United Nations is now seeking to undo.

Failure to withdraw would be harmful to the long-term good of Israel. It would, in addition to its injury to the United Nations, jeopardize the prospects of the peaceful solution of the problems of the Mid-East. This could bring incalculable ills to our friends and indeed to our nation itself. It would make infinitely more difficult the realization of the goals which I laid out in my Middle East message of January 5th to the Congress seeking to strengthen the area against Communist aggression, direct or indirect.

The United Nations must not fail. I believe that—in the interests of peace—the United Nations has no choice but to exert pressure upon Israel to comply with the withdrawal resolutions. Of course, we still hope that the Government of Israel will see that its best immediate and long-term interests lie in compliance with the United Nations and in placing its trust in the resolutions of the United Nations and in the declaration of the United States with reference to the future.

Egypt, by accepting the six principles adopted by the Security Council last October in relation to the Suez Canal, bound itself to free and open transit through the canal without discrimination and to the principle that the operation of the canal should be insulated from the politics of any country.

We should not assume that, if Israel withdraws, Egypt will prevent Israeli shipping from using the Suez Canal or the Gulf of Aqaba. If, unhappily, Egypt does hereafter violate the Armistice Agreement or other international obligations, then this should be dealt with firmly by the society of nations.

The Tasks of the United Nations

The present moment is a grave one, but we are hopeful that reason and right will prevail. Since the events of last October–November, solid progress has been made, in conformity with the charter of the United Nations. There is the cease-fire, the forces of Britain and France have been withdrawn, the forces of Israel have been partially withdrawn, and the clearing of the canal nears completion. When Israel completes its withdrawal, it will have removed a definite block to further progress.

Once this block is removed, there will be serious and creative tasks for the United Nations to perform. There needs to be respect for the right of Israel to national existence and to internal development. Complicated provisions insuring the effective international use of the Suez Canal will need to be worked out in detail. The Arab refugee problem must be solved. As I said in my special message to Congress on January 5, it must be made certain that all the Middle East is kept free from aggression and infiltration.

Finally, all who cherish freedom, including ourselves, should help the nations of the Middle East achieve their just aspirations for improving the well-being of their peoples.

What I have spoken about tonight is only one step in a long process calling for patience and diligence, but at this moment it is the critical issue on which future progress depends.

It is an issue which can be solved if only we will apply the principles of the United Nations.

That is why, my fellow Americans, I know that you want the United States to continue to use its maximum influence to sustain those principles as the world's best hope for peace.

GREAT
SPEECHES
IN
HISTORY

The Six-Day
War and Its
Aftermath

Preparing to Defend Against Israeli Aggression

George J. Tomeh

Dr. George J. Tomeh, the representative from Syria to the
United Nations in 1966 offers a justification of the military buildup in the Middle East in the fall of 1966, which
would eventually lead to war in the following June. The
Arab community had strongly opposed the creation of
the Israeli state in Palestine since its inception in 1948.
Many Arabs saw Israel as an implanted colonial state in
their territory. However, also in 1948, the United Nations
passed a resolution promising a Palestinian homeland for
displaced Palestinian Arabs. By 1966, this promise had
not been fulfilled. Further, Israel proved in its War for
Independence and the Sinai War that it was a formidable
military power supported by the United States and
Europe.

Tomeh's speech is among many made by representatives from Jordan, Saudi Arabia, Iraq, and others in support of Palestine in the face of what they considered the
racist, colonialist policies of Israel and the United States.
Dr. Tomeh's main point is redefining Zionism as a term of
oppression. He continues with the plight of the Palestinian
refugees, demanding just compensation for their losses, as
compared to the seemingly paltry concessions found in the
Israeli and international plans. Finally he notes how it is
nearly impossible for Arab countries in the Middle East to
defend themselves against potential hostilities when Israel
is being given (or sold at bargain prices) huge amounts of
armaments from the largest world power. The Arabs have

George J. Tomeh, statement before the United Nations, October 18, 1966.

no other choice, he finally concludes, than to build up
their own military cache, depriving their own citizens of
the critical aid in order to defend themselves from the possible Israeli aggression.

Pretexts are always being used to justify subjugation of
the people of Asia and Africa. Is not Southern Rhode-
sian neo-colonialism a case in point? What else is the
justification for the presence of a minority in Rhodesia which
subjects the country to its will by force of arms while preventing the overwhelming majority of the population from
exercising their right to independence and freedom? In addition to all this, the racist white régime in Rhodesia has declared unilaterally its independence, in defiance of world
public opinion, moral and human values and the principles
of international law.

Colonialism in the Middle East

In this connexion, how does Israel differ from the régime established in Southern Rhodesia? Here, too, a foreign minority, brought to Palestine from the four corners of the earth,
has been afforded the means—in complicity with the colonialist Powers—to impose its will on the inhabitants of the
country. As a result of this colonialist venture, a whole people
has been dispossessed and expelled from its homeland.

The pretext to justify this unparalleled aggression has
been that the Jews lived in Palestine some two thousand
years ago. Were we to accept this fallacy, the map of the
world would be completely changed. Indeed, the continued
presence of Portuguese colonialism in Africa is nothing but a
manifestation of colonial rule based on sheer brute force.
This lamentable state of affairs continues in defiance of the
Declaration of Independence adopted by the General Assembly at its fifteenth session calling for the liquidation of colonialism everywhere in the world. A Special Committee was
then established whose mandate was to implement the resolution. Syria feels honoured to be a member of this Special

Committee, which we think has achieved a notable record and contributed greatly to the cause of liberty in the world.

Colonialism, cunning as it is, offers false pretexts to justify its unwillingness to abide by the resolution and grant freedom to its colonies, thus depriving the colonial peoples of the enjoyment of their lawful right to independence and emancipation.

What is happening today in Aden, Oman and Southern Arabia, where brave freedom-fighters are massacred simply because they claim their inalienable rights, is in fact an example of colonialist tyranny, which no United Nations resolutions, code of human rights, or considerations of justice or morality restrain. The embittered struggle for independence in the southern part of the Arabian Peninsula bears witness to British colonialism, which has delayed its awaited departure from the area and has thus far violated United Nations resolutions calling for the ending of colonialism there. The establishment of new military British bases in Musqat and other Sheikhdoms on the Arabian Gulf proves beyond doubt that the British Government is flouting the resolutions of our Organization. This colonialist obstinacy only strengthens our demand that British troops be evacuated immediately from the region. There is no reason why the people of the area should continue to be deprived of decent life and liberty, and the colonial propaganda attempting to convey to the outside world that the colonialist presence is the forerunner of progress does not deceive anybody in this enlightened age.

Emerging nations are threatened today by various types of colonial and neo-colonial forms of economic penetration, where advantage is taken of the need of the developing countries, which have recently achieved independence, to secure assistance or technical help. It is through these channels that neo-colonialism attempts to re-establish its position of power and control.

The Threat of Zionism

While we express these views on imperialism and colonialism and the various means which they employ to gain control in the developing countries, we find that the Zionist occupation of Palestine constitutes one of the highest peaks attained by both colonialism and imperialism. On the one hand, Zionism employs all the methods of old colonialism through occupation of a land, expulsion of its people and confiscation of its property, while on the other hand Israel plays the role of benevolent provider, when it is in fact an imperialist tool, commissioned by imperialist countries to grant loans and extend assistance in their name.

The conspiracy of Israel with the imperialist countries is not limited to economic matters. It has been proved beyond doubt that Israel has cooperated with colonialist Powers and interests in many of the countries struggling to achieve independence. The records of the United Nations abound in instances in which the delegation of Israel has taken a negative stand on the struggle of African countries for emancipation.

To these instances we can add recent proof of this persistent Israeli attitude. News coming directly from Israel indicated that General Moshe Dayan, former Israeli Chief of Staff, went to South Viet-Nam to assist its Government in its aggressive war against the Army of National Liberation, the FNL. He went there disguised as a war correspondent in order to conceal the real nature of his assignment. It has also been proved beyond doubt that Israel has supplied the Portuguese army in Angola with armaments of Israeli manufacture. This fact came to light when the People's Movement for the Liberation of Angola (MPLA) issued a press release in Dar es Salaam on 6 May last, which I quote:

"The Angolan people, fighting against colonial domination and for independence, are going on to an inevitable victory. However, this struggle is made difficult by the imperialist countries and their agents who give enormous assistance to the fascist government of Portugal.

"On 24 March, 1966 a detachment of guerillas of the MPLA, acting in the Angolan region of Cabinda, destroyed a unit of the Portuguese colonial army and captured a lot of war material. Among the material captured were several submachine guns UZ3, made in Israel.

"This fact proves that Israel is furnishing war material to

the Portuguese colonialists for the extermination of the Angolan people fighting for their independence. In the same way that the imperialist Governments co-operate with Portugal in NATO, Israel is giving military assistance to the colonialists and thus contributes to the protraction of the colonial régime in Angola and the slavery of the African people.

"The MPLA denounces this and strongly protests against this co-operation between Israel and the Portuguese colonialists."

Palestine

As a matter of actual fact, the unrest and disturbances to which the Middle East has been exposed for eighteen years has been entirely due to the carving out of a part of the Arab homeland in Palestine, to be presented as a free gift by the Western nations—headed by Britain and the United States of America—for the creation of what today is called Israel. Strangers brought from various parts of the world occupy the place of the Arab people of Palestine, who have been expelled from their homeland in the ugliest and most brutal manner ever resorted to in the twentieth century. In truth, occupation by Jews from foreign countries of the place of a people settled in its homeland, and the setting up of a usurping authority on the lands of this exiled people is an occurrence without parallel in contemporary history. This was coupled with the most shameful implications of domination and colonialism, using the instruments of destruction, oppression and expulsion.

The element invading Palestine was not content with occupation, with the help of colonialist countries and the protection of their soldiers, but went on to drive out most of the inhabitants, confiscate their possessions, and deal with the remaining Arab minority in a way comparable to the régimes of racist discrimination in South Africa and Rhodesia in all its rigour and brutality.

Ever since the Zionist occupation of Palestine, eighteen years ago, the Israeli authorities, in complicity with and having the full support and financial and military co-operation of the colonialist Powers, have persisted in engendering crisis after crisis, and in creating tension by committing one act of aggression after another against the Arab countries along the demarcation lines.

Here one may be able to form an idea of the extreme tension created in the area subsequent to the forceful injection of this alien presence in the Arab world. Suffice it to mention that one fifth of all Security Council meetings has been devoted to the discussion of Israeli aggressions against Arab countries, and that various pertinent United Nations organs and the Mixed Armistice Commissions have received over 4,000 complaints involving aggressive acts committed by Israel. All this is happening while the rightful people of occupied Palestine continue to live under tents, exposed to the ravages of hunger and disease, deprived of property and homeland and of opportunity to avail themselves of the right of self-determination, freedom and independence, available to all the peoples of the world.

Refugees

The expelled people of Palestine are scattered all over the four countries bordering their homeland. These are Syria, Lebanon, Jordan and the United Arab Republic. The total number of the Palestinian victims of Israeli aggression exceeds one and a half million. Although the United Nations established the United Nations Relief and Works Agency (UNRWA) over seventeen years ago to attend to the needs of the refugees, to feed them and care for their health and education, one is astonished to learn of the meagre budget available to this organization. Yet every year we are informed that one country or another plans to reduce its contribution to the budget of UNRWA.

The threats to reduce contributions are but another means of pressure used to liquidate one of the last rights remaining to this oppressed people, and are further proof of the degree of dissipation of the principles of justice in colonialist countries—which so often lecture us in the floweriest terms of the virtues of freedom and democracy, while the sufferings of entire nations and peoples, such as Palestine and other occupied and subjugated areas in Africa and Asia, sit but lightly on their conscience.

Imagine that what is allocated to feed the Palestinian refugees does not exceed $1.2l per person per month. This sadly surprising sum is about to be reduced even further, and half the refugees now do not get even that sum; while children of the refugees, who were born after the tragedy, are not even entitled to receive the benefits of this measly figure.

But the Arab people of Palestine are neither poor nor helpless. When they were forced out of their homeland by the terrorist Zionist gangs, supported by international colonialism, they left behind properties worth $2,000 million, with a yearly income estimated, according to experts, at $173 million. If we add to that the accumulated interest of this sum for the last eighteen years, we find that the people of Palestine do not need either American or any other kind of assistance, for they do not wish to live as recipients of international charity.

The Role of the United States

The Palestine Arab expellees have requested that they be granted the income accruing to them from their properties, which totals yearly five times the present expenditure of UNRWA. When the Arab States requested that the United Nations appoint an international custodian for these properties, who would supervise the collection of the income with the assistance of international civil servants, so that it might be disbursed for the benefit of the refugees, the United States was amongst the first countries to oppose this proposal. Had such a custodian been appointed, the United States and other countries would have been spared the necessity of making a contribution to the UNRWA budget.

American support for Israel is not confined to this area alone. Rather, the United States takes it upon itself to supply Israel with all the means of committing aggression and inflicting destruction. Israel has received from the United States this year over 200 M-48 Patton tanks, and 90 F-104 jet planes and a number of Hawk missiles of the type used in the

United States Army and the armies of its allies in NATO.

I wish to assure the representatives here that Israel is in no financial position to pay the cost of these weapons of aggression. They should also not be surprised to learn that these armaments have been supplied to the authorities of Palestine at a nominal cost; so nominal that the American Secretary of Defense did not disclose the price of these armaments when he was testifying before the Senate Foreign Relations Committee. Divulging the fantastically low price would have no doubt uncovered the scandal and conspiracy involved.

The Israeli Threat

What is the inevitable purpose of Israel's possession of this military potential, in addition to the enormous amounts of war materials in its arsenal? It is aggression. In the period that has elapsed since the last session of the General Assembly, Israel has committed two very dangerous aggressions on the Truce demarcation lines which separate the Syrian Arab Republic from the Israeli occupied area of Palestine. The first was committed on 14 July 1966, when several squadrons of Israeli bombers and fighters attacked and bombed an engineering development project located on one of the tributaries of the River Jordan inside Syrian territory, killing and wounding innocent civilians. The second was when its armed gunboats fired at Syrian positions on the shores of Lake Tiberias on 15 August 1966, an action which necessitated counter action by Syrian forces as a measure of self-defence.

While unveiling these details of Israeli aggression before the Assembly, we wish to announce from this international rostrum that the establishment of Israel in the heart of the Arab homeland is intended to divide the Arab world in Asia from the Arab world in Africa, and to use it as a frontline colonial base in this area of the world, where a voluminous amount of armaments and ammunition can be assembled and placed at the disposal of the imperialist Powers, who will use it to prevent the unification of the Arab world and hinder its progress and development.

The Syrian Arab Republic, along with all the other Arab countries, is constantly directing attention to the inherent dangers emanating from the creation of Israel as a colonial outpost in the Middle East. We do so because we are convinced that world public opinion is gradually realizing the factual objectives for which it was created. The clever concealment of these facts behind the curtain of the tragedies that befell the Jewish people was intended only to camouflage the real plans of the founders of this usurper State and those of the countries which assisted in the fulfilment of these plans. We shall not allow any opportunity to slip by without directing the attention of the whole world to the potential dangers that may engulf the area should this Israeli travesty be permitted to continue.

When we speak of the dangers which Israel poses to the peace, it is because these dangers do not threaten the Middle East alone, but they are likely to spread to other regions of the world. The basic philosophy which was at the foundation of the establishment of Israel is in actual point of fact a racist, aggressive and expansionist philosophy. The slogans and doctrines laid down, assembled and disseminated in books written and published by an earlier generation of Zionists are to be found in Israel today without discontinuity in the expressions and speeches and party platforms of their leaders. All these doctrines preach expansion, aggression, and the usurpation of additional Arab territories, extending from the Nile to the Euphrates.

The Arab States today do not merely confront the 2 million Zionists who live in Israel, but, rather, they confront an organized worldwide Zionist movement entrenched in an overwhelming number of Western States, especially in the United States, where it is supported by the most influential political and governmental leaders. In addition to this, colonial countries have made their support of Israel against the Arab States a cardinal principle in the pursuit of their internal and external policies. This is what draws the lines of the confrontation between us and Zionism, and throws light on the immensity of the obstacles in the way of the achievement of unity and development by the Arab States.

The majority of the countries which belong to the emerging nations in the world are heavily handicapped by burdens of poor conditions left behind by colonialism, which during its occupation of our lands pursued the one selfish objective of imposing its authority, draining of our natural resources, and restraining by all means at their disposal our efforts to develop and progress. The colonialists embarked on this course out of fear that our development and progress would pose a threat to its controls and interests in our domains. And when movements of national liberation were organized with the admitted purpose of overthrowing foreign rule in the respective countries and forcing it to relinquish its control and depart forever, they were confronted by obstacles of enormous magnitude. But the courage displayed by the colonized peoples and the support that the peoples gave to these movements of national liberation overcame all the shortcomings and enabled them gradually to go forward and conquer whatever impediments that stood in the way.

In the Middle East, however, the problems that faced the Arab States were more complicated and infinitely more difficult, for in their struggle to rid themselves of colonialism they found themselves on the eve of independence to be facing the same obstacles which had confronted all developing countries, in addition to the heavy and very bloody burdens which colonialism left behind when it created the alien State of Israel.

The Arab countries were plagued and confronted by a disease in their midst which fortunately other countries which had emerged from the darkness of colonialism and into the bright light of liberty did not have to face. This unique situation confronts the Arab States which, though they share no responsibility for creating it, have had none the less to devote a great portion of their very limited material potential to strengthening their defences so as to be able to defend their sovereignty from the aggressive and expansionist Zionist dangers threatening the area.

The diversion of a large percentage of our national income to the area of defence has deprived our people, who are the source of this income, from the benefits that would have accrued to them had we been able to spend it on much needed development projects. While these great burdens beset our people, we note that Israel continues to receive billions of dollars and unlimited quantities and varieties of arms and ammunition from Western sources at a nominal price.

Rallying Egypt for War

Gamal Abdel Nasser

Gamal Abdel Nasser became president of Egypt in 1956 and immediately engaged his country in the Sinai War against what he called "the tripartite aggression," or the imperialist powers of England, France, and Israel. Egypt was soundly defeated in the fight. Unwilling to accept total defeat, Nasser addressed the following speech to his people and his military in May 1967. He asserts that Israel did not have the military victory it claimed in the Sinai War and rallies his forces for a new conflict. This would become the Six-Day War of June 1967, possibly the most contentious war in the Arab-Israeli conflict. Noting the military build-up, Israel launched a pre-emptive strike and soundly defeated the collective forces of Egypt and several other Arab countries that had amassed to destroy the Jewish state. As a result, Israel took control of a vast amount of new territory.

Many consider Nasser's actions in May 1967, including this speech, directly responsible for leading to the war. Besides ensuring the support of the other Arab leaders, including a reluctant King Hussein of Jordan, he evicted the United Nations Emergency Forces (UNEF) from the Sinai region and reinstated his own military there. He also blockaded the Strait of Tiran, disallowing Israel access to the Gulf of Aqaba. (Israel considered this a declaration of war.)

In the May speech, Nasser paints Israel as the aggressor in Middle Eastern conflict. He claims it is threatening Syria's interests in the Golan Heights and ignoring the plight of the Palestinians. Anticipating international reaction, Nasser asserts that UN resolutions have never benefited Arabs, and the few positive suggestions, such as partitioning the region into separate Israeli and Palestinian states, have never been implemented by Israel or pursued by western powers. Finally, he speaks to creating a new pan-Arab alliance, arguing for a tighter anti-Israel platform for all Arab nations.

The entire country looks up to you today. The entire Arab nation supports you. It is clear that in these circumstances the entire people fully support you and consider the armed forces as their hope today. It is definite that the entire Arab nation also supports our armed forces in the present circumstances through which the entire Arab nation is passing.

What I wish to say is that we are now in 1967, and not in 1956 after the tripartite aggression. A great deal was said and all the secrets were ambiguous. Israel, its commanders and rulers, boasted a great deal after 1956. I have read every word written about the 1956 events, and I also know exactly what happened in 1956.

The Sinai War

On the night of Oct. 29, 1956, the Israeli aggression against us began. Fighting began on Oct. 30. We received the Anglo-French ultimatum which asked us to withdraw several miles west of the Suez Canal.

On Oct. 31, the Anglo-French attack on us began. The air raids began at sunset on Oct. 31. At the same time, all our forces in Sinai were withdrawn completely to inside Egypt. Thus in 1956 we did not have an opportunity to fight Israel. We decided to withdraw before the actual fighting with Israel began.

Despite our decision to withdraw, Israel was unable to

occupy any of our positions except after we left them. But Israel created a big uproar, boasted and said a great deal about the Sinai campaign and the Sinai battle.

Every one of you knows all the rubbish that was said. They probably believed it themselves.

Today, more than 10 years after Suez, all the secrets have been exposed. The most important secret concerns [Israeli prime minister David] Ben-Gurion, when the imperialists brought him to France to employ him as a dog for imperialism to begin the operation.

Ben-Gurion refused to undertake anything unless he was given a written guarantee that they would protect him from the Egyptian bombers and the Egyptian Air Force. All this is no longer secret. The entire world knows.

It was on this basis that France sent fighter planes to Ben-Gurion, and it was also on this basis that Britain pledged to Ben-Gurion to bomb Egyptian airfields within 24 hours after the aggression began.

This goes to show how much they took into account the Egyptian forces. Ben-Gurion himself said he had to think about the Haifa-Jerusalem-Tel Aviv triangle, which contains one-third of Israel's population. He could not attack Egypt out of fear of the Egyptian Air Force and bombers.

At that time we had a few [Russian made] Ilyushin bombers. We had just acquired them to arm ourselves. Today we have many Ilyushins and others. There is a great difference between yesterday and today, between 1956 and 1967.

An Opportunity for Egypt

Why do I say all this? I say it because we are in a confrontation with Israel. Israel today is not backed by Britain and France as was the case in 1956. It has the United States, which supports it and supplies it with arms. But the world cannot again accept the plotting which took place in 1956.

Israel has been clamoring since 1956. It speaks of Israel's competence and high standard of training. It is backed in this by the West and the Western press. They capitalized on the Sinai campaign, where no fighting actually took place because we had withdrawn to confront Britain and France.

Today we have a chance to prove the fact. We have, indeed, a chance to make the world see matters in their true perspective. We are now face to face with Israel. In recent days Israel has been making threats of aggression and it has been boasting.

On May 12 a very impertinent statement was made. Anyone reading this statement must believe that these people are so boastful and deceitful that one simply cannot remain silent. The statement said that the Israeli commanders have announced they would carry out military operations against Syria in order to occupy Damascus and overthrow the Syrian Government.

On the same day, Israeli Premier Eshkol made a strongly threatening statement against Syria. At the same time, the commentaries said that Israel believed Egypt could not make a move because it was bogged down in Yemen.

Of course they say that we are bogged down in Yemen and have problems there. We are in Yemen. But they seem to believe the lies they have been saying all these years about our existence in Yemen. It is also possible that the Israelis believe such lies.

We are capable of bearing our duties in Yemen, and at the same time doing our national duty here in Egypt in defending our borders and in attacking if Israel attacks Arab country.

On May 13 we received accurate information that Israel was concentrating on the Syrian border huge armed forces of about 11 to 13 brigades. These forces were divided into two fronts, one south of Lake Tiberias and the other north of the lake.

The decision made by Israel at this time was to carry out an aggression against Syria as of May 17. On May 14 we took our measures, discussed the matter and contacted our Syrian brothers. The Syrians also had this information.

On this basis, Lieut. Gen. Mahmud Fawzi left for Syria to coordinate matters. We told them that we had decided that if Syria was attacked, Egypt would enter the battle from the first minute. This was the situation May 14. The forces began to move in the direction of Sinai to take up normal positions.

News agencies reported yesterday that these military movements must have been the result of a previously well-laid plan. And I say that the sequence of events determined the plan. We had no plan before May 13, because we believed that Israel would not dare attack any Arab country and that Israel would not have dared to make such an impertinent statement.

The U.N.E.F.

On May 16 we requested the withdrawal of the United Nations Emergency Force (U.N.E.F.) in a letter from Lieut. Gen. Mahmud Fawzi. We then requested the complete withdrawal of U.N.E.F.

A big worldwide campaign, led by the United States, Britain and Canada, began opposing the withdrawal of U.N.E.F. from Egypt. Thus we felt that there were attempts to turn U.N.E.F. into a force serving neoimperialism.

It is obvious that U.N.E.F. entered Egypt with our approval and therefore cannot continue to stay in Egypt except with our approval. Until yesterday, a great deal was said about U.N.E.F.

A campaign is also being mounted against the United Nations Secretary General because he made a faithful and honest decision and could not surrender to the pressure brought to bear upon him by the United States, Britain and Canada to make U.N.E.F. an instrument for implementing imperialism's plans.

It is quite natural—and I say this quite frankly—that had U.N.E.F. ignored its basic mission and turned to achieving the aims of imperialism, we would have regarded it as a hostile force and forcibly disarmed it. We are definitely capable of doing such a job.

I say this now not to discredit the U.N.E.F. but to those who have neoimperialist ideas and who want the United Nations to achieve their aims: There is not a single nation which truly respects itself and enjoys full sovereignty which could accept these methods in any form.

At the same time I say that the U.N.E.F. has honorably and faithfully carried out its duties. And the U.N. Secretary General refused to succumb to pressure. Thus he issued immediate orders to the U.N.E.F. to withdraw. Consequently, we laud the U.N.E.F., which stayed 10 years in our country serving peace.

And when they left—at a time when we found that the neoimperialist forces wanted to divert them from their basic aim—we gave them a cheerful sendoff and saluted them.

Peace in the Region?

Our forces are now in Sinai, and we are in a state of complete mobilization in Gaza and Sinai. We note that there is a great deal of talk about peace these days. Peace, peace, international peace, international security, U.N. intervention and so on and so forth, which appears daily in the press.

Why is it that no one spoke about peace, the United Nations and security when on May 12 the Israeli Premier and the Israeli commanders made their statements that they would occupy Damascus, overthrow the Syrian region, strike vigorously at Syria and occupy a part of Syrian territory?

It was obvious that they approved of the statements made by the Israeli Premier and commanders.

There is talk about peace now. What is peace? If there is a true desire for peace, we say that we also work for peace.

But does peace mean that we should ignore the rights of the Palestinian people because of the lapse of time? Does peace mean that we should concede our rights because of the lapse of time? Nowadays they speak about a "U.N. presence in the region for the sake of peace." Does "U.N. presence in the region for peace" mean that we should close our eyes to everything?

The United Nations adopted a number of resolutions in favor of the Palestinian people. Israel implemented none of these resolutions. This brought no reaction from the United States.

Today U.S. Senators, members of the House of Representatives, the press and the entire world speak in favor of Israel, of the Jews. But nothing is said in favor of the Arabs.

The U.N. resolutions which are in favor of the Arabs were not implemented. What does this mean? No one is speaking in the Arab's favor. How does the United Nations stand with regard to the Palestinian people? How does it stand with regard to the tragedy which has continued since 1958?

The peace talk is heard only when Israel is in danger. But when Arab rights and the rights of the Palestinian people are lost, no one speaks about peace, rights or anything.

Therefore it is clear that an alliance exists between the Western powers—chiefly represented by the United States and Britain—and Israel. There is a political alliance. This political alliance prompts the Western powers to give military equipment to Israel.

We Are Ready for War

Yesterday and the day before yesterday the entire world was speaking about Sharm el Sheik, navigation in the Gulf of Aqaba, the Elath port. This morning I heard the B.B.C. say that in 1956 Abdel Nasser pledged to open the Gulf of Aqaba.

Of course this is not true. It was copied from a British paper called The Daily Mail. No such thing happened. Abdel Nasser would never forfeit any United Arab Republic (U.A.R.) right. As I said, we would never give away a grain of sand from our soil or our country.

The armed forces' responsibility is now yours. The armed forces yesterday occupied Sharm el Sheik. What is the meaning of the armed force's occupation of Sharm el Sheik? It is an affirmation of our rights and our sovereignty over the Aqaba Gulf. The Aqaba Gulf constitutes our Egyptian territorial waters. Under no circumstances will we allow the Israeli flag to pass through the Aqaba Gulf.

The Jews threatened war. We tell them: You are welcome, we are ready for war. Our armed forces and all our people are ready for war, but under no circumstances will we abandon any of our rights. This water is ours.

War might be an opportunity for the Jews—for Israel and Rabin [Maj. Gen. Itzhak Rabin, the Chief of Staff]—to test their forces against ours and to see that what they wrote about the 1956 battle and the occupation of Sinai was all a lot of nonsense.

Of course there is imperialism, Israel and reaction. Reaction casts doubt on everything, and so does the Islamic alliance.

We all know that the Islamic Alliance is now represented

by three states: the kingdom of Saudi Arabia, the kingdom of Jordan, and Iran. They are saying that the purpose of the Islamic Alliance is to unite the Moslems against Israel.

I would like the Islamic Alliance to serve the Palestine question in only one way: by preventing the supply of oil to Israel. The oil which now reaches Israel through Elath comes from one of the Islamic Alliance states. It goes to Elath from Iran.

Who is supplying Israel with oil? The Islamic Alliance-Iran, an Islamic Alliance state.

Such is the Islamic Alliance. It is an imperialist alliance, and this means it sides with Zionism because Zionism is the main ally of imperialism.

The Arab world, which is now mobilized to the highest degree, knows all this. It knows how to deal with the imperialist agents, the allies of Zionism and the fifth column. They say they want to coordinate their plans with us. We cannot at all coordinate our plans with the Islamic Alliance members because it would mean giving our plans to the Jews and to Israel.

This is a serious battle. When we said we were ready for the battle, we meant that we would indeed fight if Syria or any other Arab state was subjected to aggression.

The armed forces are now everywhere. The army and all the forces are now mobilized, and so are the people. They are all behind you, praying for you day and night and feeling that you are the pride of their nation, of the Arab nation. This is the feeling of the Arab people in Egypt and outside Egypt. We are confident that you will honor the trust.

Every one of us is ready to die and not give away a grain of his country's sand. This, for us, is the greatest honor. It is the greatest honor for us to defend our country. We are not scared by imperialist, Zionist or reactionary campaigns.

We are independent and we know the taste of freedom. We have built a strong national army and achieved our objectives. We are building our country.

There is currently a propaganda campaign, a psychological campaign and a campaign of doubt against us. We leave all this behind us and follow the course of duty and victory.

May God be with you!

Victory Has Unified and Strengthened Israel

Levi Eshkol

Levi Eshkol replaced David Ben-Gurion as prime minister of Israel in 1963. In 1966, Israel suffered several attacks from Syrian guerrillas. Emboldened by their success, Syria joined with Egypt (with the aid of Soviet arms and supplies) to mobilize a military force against Israel. Egypt, under Gamal Abdul Nasser, enlisted the support of Iraq. Jordan, while urged by Israel not to join the alliance, also joined with Nasser and the other Arab states. While Egypt was beginning to amass troops at the Israel border, Israel launched a pre-emptive strike, destroying almost the entire fleet of the Egyptian Air Force while still on the ground. Guaranteed air superiority, Israel quickly defeated the Syrian and Jordanian forces and seized the areas of the Sinai Peninsula, the Gaza Strip, the West Bank, the Golan Heights, and all of Jerusalem.

Eshkol, considered one of the more peaceful of Israeli prime ministers and typically against the conquest of Arab land, annexed East Jerusalem after the war and claimed the entire city for Israel. In this speech to the Knesset (Israel's Parliament) he sees a united Jerusalem as integral to a united Israel, noting the reclaiming of Jewish holy sites such as the Western Wall and the Cave of Machpela in Hebron. This further raised the ire of the Arab states as these are also important Muslim holy sites. The powerful emotional, religious, and cultural impact of these sites is evident in Eshkol's address. After the Six-Day War, the

Levi Eshkol, statement to the Knesset, June 12, 1967.

United Nations passed resolutions 242 and 338 stating Israel should relinquish all territories acquired in the conflict and withdraw to the pre-1967 borders, and for the Arab countries to recognize and respect Israeli statehood. These resolutions have never been fully implemented.

A week ago the momentous struggle opened. The existence of the State of Israel, the hope of generations and vision that has been realized in our days, hung in the balance.

Now, only a week after the last session of the Knesset, which took place to the accompaniment of the thunder of guns, we meet with the tidings of victory ringing in our ears. . . .

Jerusalem Is One City Again

Jerusalem has been reunified. For the first time since the establishment of the State, Jews can pray at the Western Wall, the relic of our holy Temple and our historic past, and at Rachel's Tomb. For the first time in our generation, Jews can pray at the Cave of the Machpela in Hebron, the city of the Patriarchs. The prophecy has been fulfilled: "There is recompense for the work, the sons have returned to their borders."

Now that victory has been won, let us bow our heads in reverent memory of the fallen. Hundreds of soldiers of the Israel Defense Forces and civilians have given their lives for this victory. I know that there can be no consolation for the loss of the individual and the bereavement of a family. Every living soul is an entire universe. Let all the bereaved families know that there can be no cause more just and vital than that for which the dead have fought. Let them know that by their deaths they bequeathed life to all of us. In the name of the entire nation, in the name of the Government and in my own, I assure them that we share in their grievous sorrow.

Our people stood the test because it was united, because at the fateful hour it was able to concentrate its efforts and act as one man.

The people stood the test. Hundreds of thousands of

young people and new immigrants, in big or little tasks, each according to his age and his abilities, proved that their roots in this country are eternal. It was shown that the spirit of the people flows from the spiritual revival of the State.

A United Israel

We saw clearly that this is no mere ingathering of the exiles, but a new—yet ancient—nation, a united nation, which has been tempered in the furnace of one Israel, forged out of all our tribes and the remnants of scattered communities—they, their sons and daughters. A nation has come into being which is ready for any effort or sacrifice in order to achieve its goals.

The State of Israel has stood the test because it knew that it carried the hopes of the entire Jewish people. The unity of our people has been forged anew in these days. All the Diaspora communities [Jews living outside of Israel] were keenly conscious of their solidarity with the State of Israel, the heart of the Jewish people. Thousands of our people came forward to help. Hundreds of thousands, millions, are ready to give us all the assistance in their power. Even those who are unable to offer their aid have their hearts with us in our struggle. Just as our own country has attained a higher unity, so has the unity of the Jewish people been reinforced. Jerusalem has been joined together, and in its unity, as our sages said, it has made all Israel brethren.

Israel has emerged stronger than before from the test of fire and blood. Faithful to herself and looking with confidence toward the future, with the aid of the Rock and Redeemer of Israel, this nation shall yet dwell in safety.

Establishing a United Arab Kingdom of Palestine and Jordan

King Hussein I

King Hussein's speech in 1972 underscores the overwhelming complexity of the Arab-Israeli conflict. The Jordanian monarch outlines plans to create a united kingdom that would include both Palestine and Jordan. Presented to both Jordanian and Palestinian dignitaries, this seems a grand, generous gesture. He acknowledges the existence of Palestine and its interests and offers to absorb it into the kingdom of Jordan despite any resistance from Israel. King Hussein I speaks of Jordan's protection of Palestine, its kinship with the people, and the deep historical connections these two entities share. He pledges a deep commitment to further protection of Palestine in the West Bank (where Israeli settlers have claimed land) under the umbrella of an Arab Kingdom led by the Jordanian monarch. Indeed, Hussein's commitment to the Palestinians, offering them citizenship, an alternative to refugee status, was more than what most Arab states proposed at the time.

However, this partnership, or absorption into Jordan, was not well received by all Palestinians. For many in Palestine, including Yasser Arafat and the Palestine Liberation Organization (PLO), this was as unacceptable as the presence of Israel. They did not want to be Jordanians. They wanted a separate, viable Palestinian state. Also, many saw Hussein's gesture as merely an attempt to

King Hussein I, "Address by King Hussein to Jordanian and Palestinian Dignitaries on March 15, 1972, Concerning Basic Principles of a Plan to Establish a United Arab Kingdom of Palestine and Jordan," *The Arab-Israeli Conflict Readings and Documents: Abridged and Revised Edition*, edited by John Norton Moore. Princeton, NJ: Princeton University Press, 1977. Copyright © 1977 by Princeton University Press. All rights reserved. Reproduced by permission.

reestablish control over territory lost in the Six-Day War—territory that Palestinians believed belonged to Palestine. This led to PLO bombings and attacks against Jordan and Syria in the 1970s. Only late into the next decade did Jordan finally relinquish control and authority of Palestinian territory back to the PLO.

M y dear brethren,
            Dear Citizens,
            It gives me great pleasure to meet with you today and to talk to you and to the nation about the affairs of the present, the past, its experiences and our aspirations and hopes for the future.

The establishment of the state of Jordan in 1921 was the most important step taken in the life of the Arab Revolution after the plot against it by its allies in the first World War was discovered. With the issue of the Balfour Declaration in 1917, the formation of the State of Jordan gained a new dimension, in that it made it possible to exclude the land east of the Jordan River from the application of the Declaration and thus save it from the Zionist schemes of that period.

In 1948 when the Arab armies entered into Palestine, the smallest among them was the "Jordan army"; yet it was able to save that part of Palestine which extends from Jenin in the north to Hebron in the south and from the Jordan River in the east to a point lying not more than 15 kilometers from the sea-shore in the west. The Jordan army was also able to save Jerusalem—the Holy Old City—in its entirety and other areas outside the city wall to the north, south and east, all of which came to be known later as Arab Jerusalem. That area which came to be known as the "West Bank" was all that remained to the Arabs from the whole of Palestine together with the narrow area now called the "Gaza strip."

A Nearly United Jerusalem

After a brief period of temporary administration, the leaders of the West Bank, and a selected group of leaders and notables, representing the Arabs of Palestine who had left their homes in the occupied territories, found the union with the East Bank was a national demand and a guarantee in the face of the constantly expanding Israeli dangers. They therefore, called for two historic conferences, the first of which convened in Jericho on 1.12.1948 and the second in Nablus on 28.12.1948. Representatives of all sections of the population including leaders and men of thought, young and old, labourers and farmers, all, attended the two conferences. Resolutions were adopted requesting His Majesty King Abdallah ibn Al-Hussein to take immediate steps to unite the two Banks into a single state under his leadership. His Majesty responded to the appeal of the nation and ordered that constitutional and practical steps be taken to realize this important national desire, which steps included that elections be held to choose legal representatives of the people of the West Bank to sit in Parliament. On April 24, 1950 the new parliament representing both Banks with its senators and deputies, held a historic session in which the first real step in contemporary Arab history was taken on the road to unity, which the Arab Revolt proclaimed on the dawn of its inception. This was achieved by the declaration of the union of the two Banks and by their fusion into one independent Arab state with a democratic parliamentary monarchy to be known as the Hashemite Kingdom of Jordan.

The union sailed in seas which were neither calm nor smooth. There were many underhanded currents stirred up by external hands attempting to create tempests in the face of the ship to force it slowly towards the rocks. But the awareness of the people in both Banks, their firm belief in the unity of their land and their recognition of the dangers lurking behind the frontiers, were the basic guarantee for the safety of the union and for its salvation from all the evils that beset it.

Foremost among the realities which the union of both Banks evolved day after day was that those living therein are one people, not two peoples. This reality became first clear when the Ansars (the supporters)—the inhabitants of the East Bank—welcomed their brethren, the Muhajereen (the Emmigrants)—the refugees from the territories of Palestine in 1948—and shared with them the loaf of bread, the root and both sweetness and bitterness of life. This fact of life was emphasized and deepened by every step the government took and was clearly reflected in everyone of its institutions: In the armed forces, in the ministries and the various government departments, this reality became clear, also in all sectors of life: be it economic, agricultural or social. . . . The day came when it was impossible for anybody to distinguish between one from the West and one from the East, unlike the way a Palestinian is distinguished from a non-Palestinian in other parts of the Arab World.

The unity of blood and destiny between the people of both Banks reached its summit in 1967 when the sons of both Banks stood on the soil of the West Bank as they did for over twenty years, kneading its sacred soil with their common blood. But the struggle was stronger than their power and circumstances were bigger than their courage. And the catastrophe occurred.

In the midst of this sea of suffering created by the June calamity the aims of the Jordan government in that period which followed the war, were summed up in two aims: the brave stand in the face of continuous and unceasing aggression against the East Bank, and the strong determination to liberate the occupied land and free our kin and brethren in the West Bank. All our efforts were directed to achieve both these goals in an atmosphere of confidence that the Arab States would support Jordan in its calamity, and with unlimited trust that the unity of Arab destiny had become a deeply rooted reality in the conscience of the whole Arab nation, a reality which cannot be shaken by regional interests however great and which cannot be reached by plans and intentions however underhanded.

And suddenly, Jordan found itself facing a new catastrophe, which if allowed to befall the country, would have resulted in the loss of the East Bank, and would have laid the stage for a final liquidation of the Palestinian case and forever. The forces setting this calamity had mobilized many elements to serve their purpose. Many other elements also fell into the nets of these forces. Many of these elements claimed the Palestinian identity of the sacred cause and thus played their roles under the guise of that name. The contradictions and conflicting currents prevailing in the world found their way into the ranks of these elements.

It was only natural that Jordan should rise up to confront the impending tragedy. The challenge was met by the stand of the unique combination of its people: the Muhajereen and the Ansars. This evil subversion was shattered on the rock of the firm national unity, as it was disintegrated by the awareness of the new man, born in 1950 who grew and flourished in the challenges which he had to face during the past twenty years.

The Suffering of Palestine

During all that period, and specially after the June war in 1967 or even before it, the leadership of Jordan was thinking about the future of the state and was planning for it. The leadership based its thinking on its faith in the message of Jordan, which message found its roots in the great Arab Revolution and its confidence in the man living on both sides of the river and his ability to play his role in serving its message and its aims.

The manner in which the fulfillment of the Palestinian cause was viewed, carried in its folds, the far reaching scope of the Arab-Israeli conflict. Palestine had always been the first goal of Zionist plans. The people of Palestine were its first victims, and were to be followed by the people of both Banks. Even if Zionist expansionism was to end at some limit, Zionist interests would only rest by keeping the Arab world weak and disunited in order to be able to safeguard its territorial gains forever. Because the opposite camp stands as one united force, it thus becomes incumbent on all Arabs to stand united also. Even more, unity in itself is not sufficient unless it comprises a real understanding encompassing all modern methods and aspects of modern development.

Jordan had always understood the magnitude of the tragedy that befell the Palestinians. After the Zionist plot had dispersed them, in 1948 no country, Arab or non-Arab, offered the Palestinians what Jordan gave them in the way of honourable life and decent living. In Jordan, and under the auspices of the union of both Banks, the genuine Palestinian community was found among the overwhelming majority of the people who live in both Banks, and in it the Palestinian found the appropriate framework in which to live and move as well as the real starting point for the will of liberation and all its hopes.

Palestinian Identity

The Palestinians had existed hundreds of years before 1948 and continue to exist since 1948. But the events which started to prevail throughout the Arab World and all the forces and currents which manipulate them started to overlook these facts and to ignore them in conformity with the state of indecision which our nation is undergoing for years. This artificial status was given further impetus by the various conferences, plots and attacks, we have been seeing and hearing of. It was as if the Palestinian was intended to dissociate himself from his national identity and to place himself in a small separate flask which could easily be destroyed at any moment. Surely, this appeared to be another plot being hatched in the long chain of plots against the people of Palestine and the whole of the Arab nation.

These suspicious movements were not directed only to the minority of the Palestinians living outside both Banks, but were also aimed at the majority here in the hope of forcing the people of the West Bank into a state which would separate them from all that surrounds them. If some of the powers that encourage these currents do not conceal their desire to abandon their responsibilities toward the Palestine cause and the Palestinian people, by pushing them into separation, yet its brilliance however attractive it may seem to them, should not conceal from us the danger of their reaching a situation which would make them an easy prey to Israel's unlimited greed. These suspicious movements try to make the Jordan rule appear as attempting to seek gains and benefits. They try to find their way into our unity in an attempt to weaken it and create doubts about it. Attempts are also being made to exploit some people's desire to obtain material gains to the extent of pushing them to play their roles to attain their ultimate vicious end.

The Israeli occupation of the West Bank and other Arab territories dear to us has managed to continue due to the disintegration of the Arab front, the lack of coordination, the struggle to establish opposing axes and camps, the abandonment of the essence of the Palestine cause and its needs, the concentration on talking in the name of the Palestine cause in place of consorted action, as well as the attempt by certain groups to attain power through internal strife. All this also led to deepen the suffering of the Palestine people and to push them into a state of utter confusion and loss. The talk about municipal elections in the West Bank is merely an example of such a tragedy which certain quarters are trying to exploit to their own interests.

Jordan's Commitment

And yet, Jordan has never ceased to call for a united front needing mobilization and coordination of efforts. Jordan has never hesitated to stretch its hand with all sincerity to all its Arab brethren in its belief in the unity of our cause and our destiny and future. Jordan did not spare any effort towards liberation, although the above realities in the Arab world retarded it. Yet the serious planning for the future of the state went on, as well the events and positions taken against this country have failed to weaken our belief in the imperativeness of our final victory in liberating the land and the people. This belief is based not only in our faith in the justice of our cause, but is also based on our faith in our country and people on both Banks of the river and in our nation as a whole.

Thus, it was decided to move with the state into a new stage based in its essence on liberation, its concept reflecting the aspiration of our people and embodying their belief in the unity of our nation and their sense of belonging to it. In addition to all that, it is based on the absolute determination to regain the legitimate rights of the Palestinian people, and is directed to place them in a position which will enable them to regain and safeguard these rights.

This was the pledge we made to give our people the right of self-determination. It is our answer to all those who chose to doubt that pledge and void it from its essence. Today that pledge will find its way to every citizen in this country and to every individual in this nation and in the world. It is now expanding to exceed the limits of words in order to face every possibility of disunity and to embody all national aims and goals.

We wish to declare that planning for the new phase has come as a result of continuous meetings, discussions and consultations which were held with the representatives and leaders of both Banks. There was unanimous consensus that the main shape of the new phase should include the best and most developed concept of a modern democratic state. In addition to that, it will help to create a new society built by a new man to become the driving force which will put us on the way to victory, progress, unity, freedom and a better life.

The United Arab Kingdom

We are pleased to announce that the basic principles of the proposed plan are:—

1. The Hashemite Kingdom of Jordan shall become a United Arab Kingdom, and shall be thus named.
2. The United Arab Kingdom shall consist of two regions:
    A. The Region of Palestine, and shall consist of the West Bank and any other Palestinian territories to be liberated where the population opts to join it.
    B. The Region of Jordan, and shall consist of the East Bank.
3. Amman shall be the central capital of the Kingdom and at the same time shall be the capital of the Region of Jordan.
4. Jerusalem shall become the capital of the Region of Palestine.
5. The King shall be the Head of the State and shall assume the central executive authority assisted by a Central Council of Ministers. The central legislative authority shall be vested in the King and in the National Assembly whose members shall be elected by direct and secret ballot. It shall have an equal number of members from each of the two regions.
6. The Central Judicial Authority shall be vested in a "Supreme Central Court."

7. The Kingdom shall have a single Armed Forces and its Supreme Commander shall be the King.

8. The responsibilities of the Central Executive Power shall be confined to matters relating to the Kingdom as a sovereign international entity insuring the safety of the union, its stability and development.

9. The Executive Power in each region shall be vested in a Governor General from the Region and in a Regional Council of Ministers also from the Region.

10. The Legislative Power in each Region shall be vested in "People's Council" which shall be elected by direct secret ballot. This Council shall elect the Governor General.

11. The Legislative Power in each region shall be vested in the courts of the region and nobody shall have any authority over it.

12. The Executive Power in each Region shall be responsible for all its matters with the exception of such matters as the constitution requires to be the responsibility of the Central Executive Power.

An Arab Homeland

It is obvious that the implementation of this proposed plan will require the necessary constitutional steps and Parliament shall be asked to draw up the new constitution of the country.

This new phase to which we look will guarantee the rearrangement of the "Jordan-Palestinian home" in a manner that will insure for it additional innate strength and thus the ability to achieve our hopes and aspirations. This plan will strengthen the joint fabric of both Banks and will satisfy the requirements of their unity and brotherhood and shall lead to deepen the sense of responsibility in the individual in both regions of the Kingdom, to best serve our cause without prejudicing any of the acquired rights of any citizen of Palestinian origin in the Region of Jordan or any citizen of Jordanian origin in the Region of Palestine. For this plan collects but does not disperse; it strengthens but does not weaken; and it unifies but does not disintegrate. It does not allow any changes in the gains that our citizens have acquired as a result of twenty years of union. Any attempt to cast doubt on all this will be tantamount to treason against the unity of the Kingdom and against the cause, the nation and the homeland. The citizen in our country has passed such experience and has achieved a level of awareness and ability which qualify him to cope with coming responsibilities with greater confidence and determination.

If ability is a bliss which should grow to become man's responsibility toward himself and toward others, if his awareness is a weapon to be used for his own good and that of others, then the time has come for our man to stand face to face with his responsibilities, to discharge them with honesty and practice them with courage and honour.

Thus, the above formula becomes a title for a new page, brilliant and firmly believing in the history of this country. Every citizen has his role and his duties. As to the armed forces, which have marched right from the beginning under the banner of the great Arab Revolution, that included and will forever include among its ranks the best elements from among the sons of both Banks, these armed forces will remain ready to receive more of our sons from both Banks, based on the highest level of efficiency, ability and organization, it shall always be open to welcome any one who wishes to serve our nation and our cause with absolute loyalty to the eternal goals of our nation.

This Arab country is the home of the cause, just as it is from the Arabs and for the Arabs. Its record of sacrifice for our nation and our cause is full and well known. Its pages were inscribed by the blood of its gallant armed forces and its free people. The more the positions taken against it, change into more positive brotherly assistance and support, the easier it will be for it to continue its glorious march of sacrifices, with more ability and hope, until it regains for our nation its rights and attains victory.

This Arab Country is the country of all, Jordanians and Palestinians alike. When we say Palestinian we mean every Palestinian be he in the East or West of this great world on condition that he should be loyal to Palestine and should belong to Palestine. Our call is for every citizen in this country to rise and play his role and shoulder his responsibilities in

this new phase, it is also addressed to every Palestinian outside Jordan to answer the call of duty, far from appearances
and free from ailments and diversion and to proceed and join
his kin and brethren along a single path based on this message, united in one front, clear in the aims, so that all should
cooperate to reach the goals of liberation and to build up the
structure to which we all aspire.

"GOD WILL AID THOSE WHO AID HIS CAUSE."

GREAT
SPEECHES
IN
HISTORY

The First
Steps
Toward
Peace

The Nine-Point Peace Plan

Abba Eban

In October, 1968, Israel's foreign minister addressed the United Nation's General Assembly and offered Israel's plan for peace in the region. This, of course, was a particularly bitter time in the conflict. Israel had just won a decisive victory in the Six-Day War months earlier. Instead of destroying the fledgling Israeli state, the Arabs lost a great deal of territory in the war, including Jerusalem and the Sinai peninsula, as Israel extended its borders far beyond the agreements of 1948. Israel also succeeded in scaling back any Arab military threat since the Arabs suffered huge losses in military hardware.

In his speech Abba Eban claims that Israel is more than willing to negotiate a peace with its Arab neighbors and is troubled by the Arab response, particularly Egypt's insistence on "no negotiations." Generally, the Israeli proposal Eban lays out seems quite magnanimous. However, there are some telling omissions in his plan. There is no explicit mention of Palestinians, only "refugees" and here, only refugees from the war, not from the original partition of Palestine. Granted, the United Arab Republic (UAR) was also not in agreement on Palestine and its fate. Eban also seems generous in his plan for Jerusalem—returning Islamic sites to the Arabs, for example. However, he ignores the existence of areas that are held sacred for multiple faiths. Still, it was a significant plan, and it covers the main points that would be debated for the next several decades.

Abba Eban, statement to the United Nations General Assembly, October 8, 1968.

Abba Eban, statement to the United Nations General Assembly, October 8, 1968.

Mr. President, my Government has decided to give the members of the United Nations a detailed account of its views on the establishment of a just and lasting peace in the Middle East. Amidst the tumult of a rancorous public debate, the deeper motives of our policy have not always been clearly perceived. A structure of peace cannot, of course, be built by speeches at this rostrum. It may, however, be useful for the parties to clarify their intentions and to draw a picture of their policies beyond the routine vocabulary in which this discussion has been held down for sixteen months.

In the interest of peace, I shall refrain from detailed comment on the polemical observations made here by Foreign Ministers of Arab States. The total and unblemished self-satisfaction with which these Ministers have spoken, the complete absence in their worlds of any self-criticism or innovation, the lack of detailed and organized comment on concrete issues—all these illustrate the inhibition which still prevents Arab Governments from thinking lucid and constructive thoughts about their relations with Israel. Indeed, the Foreign Minister of Sudan actually recommended that Israel be dismantled and its people dispersed. Here we have the oldest and most tenacious link in all human history between a people and a land. And an Arab leader speaks of Israel as though it were a temporary international exhibition to be folded up and taken away! Such intellectual frivolity and self-delusion are not heard on any other international issue.

A Twenty-Year War

Israel cannot easily forget the immense loss and burden which it has borne through the implacable hostility directed against it for twenty years, culminating in the unforgettable summer of 1967. For there has not been a Six-Day War. There has been a twenty-year war conducted by the Arab States in varying degrees of intensity with the candid hope of Israel's ruin and destruction. The issue is whether this war is now going to be ended by a final peace or merely interrupted in order to be resumed in conditions more propitious for Arab success.

Our danger in 1967 was the climax and not the whole story of our predicament. No other people has had to live all its days with a mark of interrogation hanging over its collective and individual survival. And behind Israel's quest for secure life, there is a particular and hideous legacy of wholesale death in the European slaughter-house. In May 1967, we found ourselves beset by deadly peril which we faced in utter solitude of action and responsibility. Maritime blockade, murderous incursions, military encirclement, declarations of overt war, a frenzied torrent of violent threats and a formal announcement by President Nasser [of Egypt] that the battle was joined for Israel's extinction, all came together in cumulative assault on Israel's life and security.

All the acts which fall under the widely supported definitions of aggression were simultaneously concerted against us. The universal conscience was deeply stirred. Millions across the world trembled for Israel's fate. The memory of those dark days broods over Israel's life. Our nation still lives intimately with the dangers which then confronted us. We still recall how the imminent extinction of Israel's statehood and the massacre of its population were seriously discussed across the world: in wild intoxication of spirit in Arab capitals, and with deep, but impotent, sorrow in other lands. To prevent the renewal of those dangers is the first law of our policy. The gravest danger is lest through a lassitude of spirit, or imprecision of diplomatic craftsmanship, or collapse of patience, we again revert to fragile, false and ambiguous solutions which carry within them the seed of future wars. Those of us who bear responsibility for our nation's survival and our children's lives cannot have anything to do with vague solutions which fall short of authentic and lasting peace. June 1967 must be the last of the Middle Eastern wars.

This resolve has moved our policy at every stage of the political discussion from the outbreak of hostilities to this very day.

Boundaries

In June and July 1967, the General Assembly rejected all proposals which sought to condemn Israel's resistance or to reconstruct the conditions which had led to the outbreak of war. A new milestone was reached when the Security Council adopted its unanimous Resolution on 22 November 1967. That Resolution was presented to us for our acquiescence, not as a substitute for specific agreement, but as a list of principles on which the parties could base their agreement. It was drafted, as Ambassador George Ball said on 11 September, as 'a skeleton of principles on which peace could be erected'. It was not meant to be self-executing. As Lord Caradon said on 22 November, it was not 'a call for a temporary truce or a superficial accommodation'; it reflected, as he said, a refusal 'to be associated with any so-called settlement which was only a continuation of a false truce'. Its author stated that any 'action to be taken must be within the framework of a permanent peace, and withdrawal must be to secure boundaries'. The term 'secure and recognized boundaries' had first appeared in a United States draft, the author of which pointed out that this meant something different from the old armistice demarcation lines. Secure and recognized boundaries, he said, had never existed in the Middle East. They must, therefore, be fixed by the parties in the course of the peacemaking process.

Now these were the understandings on which Israel's co-operation with Ambassador Jarring's mission was sought and obtained. Whatever our views might be on these formulations by other Governments, it has been evident at every stage that the two central issues are the establishment of a permanent peace and an agreement for the first time on the delineation of secure and recognized boundaries. These are the conditions prerequisite for any movement. It is here that the peacemaking process must begin. If these problems are solved, all the other issues mentioned in the Resolution fall into place. To seek a change in the cease-fire dispositions, without the framework of a just and lasting peace and the determination of agreed boundaries, is an irrational course for which there is no international authority or precedent. This would be a short and certain route to renewed war in conditions hostile to Israel's security and existence.

Our contacts with the Special Representative of the Secretary-General began in December 1967. At the end of that month, on 27 December, I conveyed a document to the Egyptian Foreign Minister, through Ambassador Jarring, proposing an agenda for a discussion on the establishment of a just and lasting peace. In this letter, I expressed a willingness to hear the UAR's views, and suggested that representatives of our two Governments be brought together informally in order to explore each other's intentions and to derive assurance and confidence for future contacts. In our letter we made it clear that the establishment of the boundary was fully open for negotiation and agreement.

The UAR made no reply, offered no comment, presented no counterproposals. Indeed, from that day to this, the UAR has not sent us a single document referring to or commenting on any Israeli letters.

Israel Is Willing to Negotiate

On 7 January, I conveyed to the Jordan Government, through Ambassador Jarring, a letter in which I sought to open a constructive dialogue. This letter reads in part:

> History and geography create an objective affinity of interest between the two countries. More than any other relationship between Middle Eastern States, this one involves human interests in a close degree of interdependence. A close and confident association would seem to be as necessary for Jordanian as for Israeli welfare.

> The major problems at issue between Jordan and Israel are closely interconnected. Territorial security, economic and humanitarian problems impinge directly on each other. Moreover, the political and juridical basis of this relationship is of overriding importance. If there is a prior agreement to establish relations of permanent peace, the specific problems at issue between the two countries can be effectively and honourably solved.

I went on to list the five major subjects on which we shall seek agreement. These included the establishment of the boundary and security arrangements. No reply was made to this approach.

On 12 February, I requested Ambassador Jarring to convey the following to the Governments of Egypt and Jordan:

> Israel has cooperated and will cooperate with you in your mission. We accept the Security Council's call, in its Resolution of 22 November 1967, for the promotion of agreement on the establishment of peace with secure and recognized boundaries.

> "Once agreement is reached on a peace settlement, it will be faithfully implemented by Israel.

> As I indicated to you on 1 February 1968, Israel is prepared to negotiate on all matters included in the Security Council Resolution which either side wishes to raise. Our views on the problems of peace and our interpretation of the Resolution were stated by me in the Security Council on 2 November 1967.

> The next step should be to bring the parties together. I refer to the agreement which I expressed to you on 1 February for the Special Representative of the Secretary-General to convene the two Governments.

This message elicited no response. On February 19, I communicated another message to Ambassador Jarring for transmission to Cairo. This message assured the Secretary-General's Representative of Israel's full cooperation in his efforts to promote agreement and to achieve an accepted settlement for the establishment of a just and lasting peace in accordance with his mandate under the Security Council Resolution of 22 November 1967.

It further pointed out that the UAR is aware of Israel's willingness to negotiate on all matters included in the Security Council Resolution. It drew attention to the fact that the Resolution is a framework for agreement, and that it cannot be fulfilled without a direct exchange of views and proposals leading to bilateral contractual commitments. It accepted the sponsor's view that the principles recommended for inclusion in the peace settlement are integrally linked and interdependent, and it proposed to move forward to a more substantive stage and to embark on a meaningful negotiation for achieving a just and lasting peace called for by the Security Council.

Early in March 1968, Ambassador Jarring sought our reaction on a proposal to convene Israel, the UAR and Jordan in conferences under his auspices to seek an agreed settlement in fulfilment of his mandate under the Security Council's Resolution. We were later informed that the UAR had rejected and that Jordan had not accepted this course. On 1 May, Ambassador Tekoah was empowered to indicate, in the Security Council, Israel's acceptance of the November Resolution for the promotion of agreement on the establishment of a just and lasting peace. The Israeli Representative was authorized to reaffirm that we were willing to seek agreement with each Arab State on all the matters included in the Resolution, and that we accepted the proposal of Dr. Jarring of bringing about meetings between Israel and its neighbours under his auspices in fulfilment of his mandate for the purpose of peaceful and accepted settlement.

On 29 May, after a discussion in our Cabinet, I made a statement in the Knesset proposing a method of implementing the Security Council Resolution through negotiation, agreement and the signature and application of treaty engagements to be worked out between the parties. In this, as in previous documents, it was made clear that we regarded the establishment of the boundary as a matter for negotiation and agreement.

The Arab Response

On 14 June, I was informed that this proposal had been conveyed to the UAR's Permanent Representative, who had noted it without any reaction. At the end of August, I submitted to the UAR Foreign Minister, through Ambassador Jarring, a series of ideas and viewpoints on the implications of the term "a just and final peace". This was developed in further communications early in September. To all these detailed proposals, the UAR replied declining any specific comment, and limiting itself to a general reference to the text of the Security Council's Resolution. The UAR would recite the Resolution in a declaration of acceptance without any specification of how it proposed to reach concrete agreement. During this time,

Egyptian policy was authoritatively defined by President Nasser in a formal utterance on 23 June. In that statement, the UAR President expressed willingness to attempt, as in March 1957, "a political solution" on condition that certain principles of Egyptian policy be recognized. He said:

"The following principles of Egyptian policy are immutable:

1. No negotiation with Israel
2. No peace with Israel
3. No recognition of Israel
4. No transactions will be made at the expense of Palestinian territories or the Palestinian people."

How one can build peace out of such negative and immutable principles defeats the imagination.

Mr. President, I have taken the General assembly into the knowledge of our initiatives and proposals. I leave it to my fellow delegates to judge whether their complete rejection was justified or compatible with a sincere attempt to explore the conditions of a permanent peace and to reach agreement.

In discussing the reasons for the lack of substantive progress, we cannot fail to perceive that the discussion on peace has revolved too much around semantic expressions, too little around the solution of contentious issues. There is no instance in history in which a stubborn and complex conflict has been brought to an end by the mere recitation of texts without precise agreement on the issues of which the conflict is composed. Israel has accepted the Security Council's Resolution for the establishment of a just and lasting peace and declared its readiness to negotiate agreements on all the principles mentioned therein. We hold that the Resolution should be implemented through negotiation, agreement and the joint signature and application of appropriate treaty engagements.

When the parties accept a basis for settlement—their least duty is to clarify what they mean by their acceptance.

To make identical and laconic statements with diametrically opposed motives and interpretations would come dangerously close to international deceit. All parties must say what they mean, and mean what they say. And the heart of the problem is not what we say, but what we do. The construction of a peaceful edifice requires sustained action in order to bring the vital interests of the parties into an acceptable harmony. There is no such thing as peace by incantation. Peace cannot be advanced by recitations accompanied by refusal to negotiate viable agreements. The Security Council's Resolution has not been used as an instrument for peace. It has been invoked as an obstacle and alibi to prevent the attainment of peace.

In these conditions, my Government has given intensive consideration to the steps that we should now take. Our conclusion is this. Past disappointment should not lead to present despair. The stakes are too high. While the ceasefire agreements offer important security against large-scale hostilities, they do not represent a final state of peace. They must, of course, be maintained and respected until there is peace. They must be safeguarded against erosion by military assault and murderous incursion. But at the same time, the exploration of a lasting peace should be constant. Unremitting, resilient and, above all, sincere, my Government deems the circumstances and atmosphere afforded by our presence here as congenial for a new attempt. We suggest that a new effort be made in the coming weeks to cooperate with Ambassador Jarring in his task of promoting agreements on the establishment of peace.

It is important to break out of the declaratory phase in which the differences of formulation are secondary and in any case legitimate, in order to give tangible effect to the principles whereby peace can be achieved in conformity with the central purposes of the United Nations Charter or the Security Council Resolution and with the norms of international law. Instead of a war of words, we need acts of peace.

Nine Principles for Peace

I come to enumerate the nine principles by which peace can be achieved:

1) The establishment of peace

The situation to follow the cease-fire must be a just and lasting peace, duly negotiated and contractually expressed.

Peace is not a mere absence of fighting. It is a positive

and clearly defined relationship with far-reaching political, practical and juridical consequences. We propose that the peace settlement be embodied in treaty form. It would lay down the precise conditions of our co-existence, including a map of the secure and agreed boundary. The essence of peace is that it commits both parties to the proposition that their twenty-year-old conflict is at a permanent end. Peace is much more than what is called "non-belligerency". The elimination of belligerency is one of several conditions which compose the establishment of a just and lasting peace. If there had previously been peace between the States of our area and temporary hostilities had erupted, it might have been sufficient to terminate belligerency and to return to the previously existing peace. But the Arab-Israel area has had no peace. There is nothing normal or legitimate or established to which to return. The peace structure must be built from its foundations. The parties must define affirmatively what their relations shall be, not only what they will have ceased to be. The Security Council, too, called for the establishment of peace and not for any intermediate or ambiguous or fragmentary arrangement such as that which had exploded in 1967.

2) Secure and Recognized Boundaries

Within the framework of peace, the cease-fire lines will be replaced by permanent, secure and recognized boundaries between Israel and each of the neighbouring Arab States, and the disposition of forces will be carried out in full accordance with the boundaries under the final peace. We are willing to seek agreement with each Arab State on secure and recognized boundaries within the framework of a permanent peace.

It is possible to work out a boundary settlement compatible with the security of Israel and with the honour of Arab States. After twenty years, it is time that Middle Eastern States ceased to live in temporary "demarcation lines" without the precision and permanence which can come only from the definite agreement of the States concerned. The majority of the United Nations have recognized that the only durable and reasonable solutions are agreed solutions serving the common interests of our peoples. The new peace structure in the Middle East, including the secure and recognized boundaries, must be built by Arab and Israeli hands.

3) Security Agreements

In addition to the establishment of agreed territorial boundaries, we should discuss other agreed security arrangements designed to avoid the kind of vulnerable situation which caused a breakdown of the peace in the summer of 1967. The instrument establishing peace should contain a pledge of mutual non-aggression.

4) The Open Frontier

When agreement is reached on the establishment of peace with permanent boundaries, the freedom of movement now existing in the area, especially in the Israel-Jordan sector, should be maintained and developed. It would be incongruous if our peoples were to intermingle in peaceful contact and commerce only when there is a state of war and cease-fire—and to be separated into ghettos when there is peace. We should emulate the open frontier now developing within communities of States, as in parts of Western Europe. Within this concept, we include free port facilities for Jordan on Israel's Mediterranean coast and mutual access to places of religious and historic associations.

5) Navigation

Interference with navigation in the international waterways in the area has been the symbol of the state of war and, more than once, an immediate cause of hostilities. The arrangements for guaranteeing freedom of navigation should be unreserved, precise, concrete and founded on absolute equality of rights and obligations between Israel and other littoral States.

6) Refugees

The problem of displaced populations was caused by war and can be solved by peace. On this problem I propose:

One: A conference of Middle Eastern States should be convened, together with the Governments contributing to refugee relief and the specialized agencies of the United Nations, in order to chart a five-year plan for the solution of the refugee problem in the framework of a lasting peace and the integration of refugees into productive life. This conference can be called in advance of peace negotiations.

Two: Under the peace settlement, joint refugee integration and rehabilitation commissions should be established by the signatories in order to approve agreed projects for refugee integration in the Middle East, with regional and international aid.

Three: As an interim measure, my Government has decided, in view of the forthcoming winter, to intensify and accelerate action to widen the uniting of families scheme, and to process "hardship cases" among refugees who had crossed to the East Bank during the June 1967 fighting. Moreover, permits for return which had been granted and not used can be transferred to other refugees who meet the same requirements and criteria as the original recipients.

7) Jerusalem

Israel does not seek to exercise unilateral jurisdiction in the Holy Places of Christianity and Islam. We are willing in each case to work out a status to give effect to their universal character. We would like to discuss appropriate agreements with those traditionally concerned. Our policy is that the Christian and Moslem Holy Places should come under the responsibility of those who hold them in reverence.

8) Acknowledgement and Recognition of Sovereignty, Integrity and Right to National Life

This principle, inherent in the Charter and expressed in the Security Council Resolution of November 1967, is of basic importance. It should be fulfilled through specific contractual engagements to be made by the Governments of Israel and of the Arab States to each other—by name. It follows logically that Arab Governments will withdraw all the reservations which they have expressed on adhering to international conventions, about the non-applicability of their signatures to their relations with Israel.

9) Regional Cooperation

The peace discussion should examine a common approach to some of the resources and means of communication in the region in an effort to lay foundations of a Middle Eastern community of sovereign States.

Our Efforts and Sincerity

Mr. President,

The process of exploring peace terms should follow normal precedents. There is no case in history in which conflicts have been liquidated or a transition effected from a state of war to a state of peace on the basis of a stubborn refusal by one State to meet another for negotiation. There would be nothing new in the experience and relationship of Israel and the Arab States for them to meet officially to effect a transition in their relationships. What is new and unprecedented is President Nasser's principle of "no negotiation".

In the meantime, we continue to be ready to exchange ideas and clarifications on certain matters of substance through Ambassador Jarring with any Arab Government willing to establish a just and lasting peace with Israel.

Mr. President,

I have expounded our views on peace in more detail than is usual in General Assembly debates. On each of these nine points we have elaborated detailed views and ideas which we would discuss with neighbouring States in a genuine exchange of views, in which we should, of course, consider comments and proposals from the other side. No Arab spokesman has yet addressed himself to us in similar detail on the specific and concrete issues involved in peacemaking. Behind our proposals lie much thought and planning which can bear fruit when our minds and hearts interact with those of neighbouring States.

We ask friendly Governments outside the region to appraise the spirit as well as the content of the ideas which I have here outlined. We urge the Arab Governments to ponder them in a deliberate mood, and to explore their detailed implications with us in the normal and appropriate frameworks.

The solutions which I have outlined cover all the matters mentioned in the Security Council's Resolution and would constitute the effective fulfilment of its purposes.

We base ourselves on the integral and interdependent character of the points at issue. Nothing is less fruitful than an attempt to give separate identity or precedence to any single principle of international policy, thus destroying its delicate balance.

Moreover, the obligations of Israel and the Arab States to each other are not exhausted by any single text. They are also governed by the Charter, by the traditional precepts of international law, by constructive realism and by the weight of human needs and potentialities.

Lest Arab Governments be tempted out of sheer routine to rush into impulsive rejection, let me suggest that tragedy is not what men suffer but what they miss. Time and again Arab Governments have rejected proposals today—and longed for them tomorrow. The fatal pattern is drawn across the whole period since 1947—and before. There is nothing unrealistic about a negotiated peace inspired by a sense of innovation and constructed by prudent and flexible statecraft. Indeed, all other courses are unrealistic. The idea of a solution imposed on the parties by a concert of Powers is perhaps the most unrealistic of all. The positions of the Powers have not moved any closer in the last fifteen months than have the positions of the parties themselves. Moreover, the Middle East is not an international protectorate. It is an area of sovereign States which alone have the duty and responsibility of determining the conditions of their co-existence. When the parties have reached agreement, it would be natural for their agreement to receive international support. To the Arab States, we say: "For you and us alone, the Middle East is not a distant concern, or a strategic interest, or a problem of conflict, but the cherished home in which our cultures were born, in which our nationhood was fashioned and in which we and you and all our posterity must henceforth live together in mutuality of interest and respect."

It may seem ambitious to talk of a peaceful Middle Eastern design at this moment of tension and rancour. But there is such a thing in physics as fusion at high temperatures. In political experience, too, the consciousness of peril often brings a thaw in frozen situations. In the long run, nations can prosper only by recognizing what their common interest demands. The hour is ripe for the creative adventure of peace.

Egypt Comes to Israel

Anwar el-Sadat

Anwar el-Sadat served as Egypt's president from 1970 until his assassination in 1981. Earlier in his career, he served in the military, helping to oust the monarchy from power and later as vice president to Gamal Abdul Nasser. Stridently anti-Israel, he stated in 1970, "Don't ask me to make diplomatic relations with them. Never. Never. Leave it to the coming generations to decide that, not me." These sentiments were cemented with his surprise attack on Israeli positions in 1973 while the Jewish state was observing Yom Kippur. Known as the Yom Kippur War, it proved that, while the Egyptians were driven back, the Israelis could be caught off guard. The attack served as a psychological victory for many Arabs.

However, by 1977, Sadat made a decisive turn, as evidenced by this speech to Israel's Knesset (parliament). He describes how he had made a historic promise to "go to the ends of the earth" to achieve peace in the region. Just ten days later, Israel extended an invitation to visit and he accepted. While this speech lacks specific solutions to such difficult issues as the Israeli occupation of the Sinai Peninsula, East Jerusalem, and the fate of Palestinian refugees, its impact was monumental. In visiting Jerusalem, Sadat became the first Arab leader to recognize the state of Israel. Further, in his speech he declares to the world a willingness to welcome Israel among its Arab neighbors and live with Israel in permanent peace. Along with breaking rank with his fellow Arab nations, Sadat's visit to Israel, while his nation was still engaged

Anwar el-Sadat, address before the Knesset, 1977.

in a decades-long war, posed a real danger to his person
and clearly demonstrated his courage and commitment.
After giving this speech Sadat worked with Israeli prime
minister Menachem Begin on a peace settlement. The two
met with U.S. president Jimmy Carter at Camp David
and ironed out the first peace accord between Israel and
an Arab nation. This earned both Sadat and Begin the
Nobel Peace Prize in 1978. Sadat's efforts stirred great
controversy in the Arab world, and that led to his assassination in 1981 by Islamic Fundamentalists.

I come to you today on solid ground to shape a new life
and to establish peace. We all love this land, the land of
God; we all, Moslems, Christians, and Jews, all worship
God.

Under God. God's teachings and commandments are
love, sincerity, security, and peace.

I do not blame all those who received my decision [to
travel to Israel] when I announced it to the entire world before the Egyptian People's Assembly. I do not blame all those
who received my decision with surprise and even with
amazement—some gripped even by violent surprise. Still others interpreted it as political, to camouflage my intentions of
launching a new war.

I would go so far as to tell you that one of my aides at
the presidential office contacted me at a late hour following
my return home from the People's Assembly and sounded
worried as he asked me, "Mr. President, what would be our
reaction if Israel actually extended an invitation to you?"

I replied calmly, "I would accept it immediately. I have
declared that I would go to the ends of the earth. I would go
to Israel, for I want to put before the people of Israel all the
facts."

I can see the faces of all those who were astounded by my
decision and had doubts as to the sincerity of the intentions
behind the declaration of my decision. No one could ever
conceive that the president of the biggest Arab state, which
bears the heaviest burden and the main responsibility per-

taining to the cause of war and peace in the Middle East, should declare his readiness to go to the land of the adversary while we were still in a state of war.

A Lasting Peace

Here I would go back to the big question: How can we achieve a durable peace based on justice? In my opinion, and I declare it to the whole world, from this forum, the answer is neither difficult nor is it impossible despite long years of feuds, blood, faction, strife, hatreds, and deep-rooted animosity.

The answer is not difficult, nor is it impossible, if we sincerely and faithfully follow a straight line.

You want to live with us, part of the world.

In all sincerity I tell you we welcome you among us with full security and safety. This in itself is a tremendous turning point, one of the landmarks of a decisive historical change. We used to reject you. We had our reasons and our fears, yes.

We refused to meet with you, anywhere, yes.

We were together in international conferences and organizations, and our representatives did not, and still do not, exchange greetings with you. Yes. This has happened and is still happening.

It is also true that we used to set as a precondition for any negotiations with you a mediator who would meet separately with each party.

Yes. Through this procedure, the talks of the first and second disengagement agreements took place.

Our delegates met in the first Geneva conference without exchanging direct word. Yes, this has happened.

Yet today I tell you, and I declare it to the whole world, that we accept to live with you in permanent peace based on justice. We do not want to encircle you or be encircled ourselves by destructive missiles ready for launching, nor by the shells of grudges and hatreds. . . .

I hail the Israeli voices that call for the recognition of the Palestinian people's right to achieve and safeguard peace.

Here I tell you, ladies and gentlemen, that it is no use to refrain from recognizing the Palestinian people and their right to statehood as their right of return. We, the Arabs, have faced this experience before, with you. And with the reality of the Israeli existence, the struggle which took us from war to war, from victims to more victims, until you and we have today reached the edge of a horrible abyss and a terrifying disaster unless, together, we seize this opportunity today of a durable peace based on justice.

You have to face reality bravely, as I have done. There can never be a solution to a problem by evading it or turning a deaf ear to it. Peace cannot last if attempts are made to impose fantasy concepts on which the world has turned its back and announced its unanimous call for the respect of rights and facts.

There is no need to enter a vicious circle as to Palestinian rights. It is useless to create obstacles; otherwise, the march of peace will be impeded or peace will be blown up. As I have told you, there is no happiness based on the detriment of others.

Direct confrontation and straightforwardness are the shortcuts and the most successful way to reach a clear objective. Direct confrontation concerning the Palestinian problem and tackling it in one single language with a view to achieving a durable and just peace lie in the establishment of that peace. With all the guarantees you demand, there should be no fear of a newly born state that needs the assistance of all countries of the world.

When the bells of peace ring, there will be no hands to beat the drums of war. Even if they existed, they would be stilled. . . .

An End to Suffering

Ladies and gentlemen, peace is not a mere endorsement of written lines. Rather, it is a rewriting of history. Peace is not a game of calling for peace to defend certain whims or hide certain admissions. Peace in its essence is a dire struggle against all and every ambition and whim.

Perhaps the example taken and experienced, taken from ancient and modern history, teaches that missiles, warships, and nuclear weapons cannot establish security. Instead, they destroy what peace and security build.

For the sake of our peoples and for the sake of the civilization made by man, we have to defend man everywhere against rule by the force of arms so that we may endow the full of humanity with all the power of the values and principles that further the sublime position of mankind.

Allow me to address my call from this rostrum to the people of Israel. I tell them, from the Egyptian people, who bless this sacred mission of peace, I convey to you the message of peace of the Egyptian people, who do not harbor fanaticism and whose sons—Moslems, Christians and Jews—live together in a state of cordiality, love, and tolerance.

This is Egypt, whose people have entrusted me with their sacred message. A message of security, safety, and peace to every man, woman, and child in Israel. Let all endeavors be channeled toward building a huge stronghold for peace instead of building destructive rockets.

Introduce to the entire world the image of the new man in this area so that he might set an example to the man of our age, the man of peace everywhere. Ring the bells for your sons. Tell them that those wars were the last of wars and the end of sorrows. Tell them that we are entering upon a new beginning, a new life, a life of love, prosperity, freedom, and peace.

You, sorrowing mother, you, widowed wife, you, the son who lost a brother or a father, all the victims of wars, fill the air and space with recitals of peace, fill bosoms and hearts with the aspirations of peace. Make a reality that blossoms and lives. Make hope a code of conduct and endeavor.

The will of peoples is part of the will of God. Ladies and gentlemen, before I came to this place, with every beat of my heart and with every sentiment, I prayed to God Almighty. While performing the prayers at the Al Aksa mosque and while visiting the Holy Sepulcher I asked the Almighty to give me strength and to confirm my belief that this visit may achieve the objective I look forward to for a happy present and a happier future.

Putting Forward the Peace Initiative

I have chosen to set aside all precedents and traditions known by warring countries. In spite of the fact that occupation of Arab territories is still there, the declaration of my readiness to proceed to Israel came as a great surprise that stirred many feelings and confounded many minds. Some of them even doubted its intent.

Despite all that, the decision was inspired by all the clarity and purity of belief and with all the true passions of my people's will and intentions, and I have chosen this road considered by many to be the most difficult road.

I have chosen to come to you with an open heart and an open mind. I have chosen to give this great impetus to all international efforts exerted for peace. I have chosen to present to you, in your own home, the realities, devoid of any scheme or whim. Not to maneuver, or win a round, but for us to win together the most dangerous of rounds embattled in modern history, the battle of permanent peace based on justice.

It is not my battle alone. Nor is it the battle of the leadership in Israel alone. It is the battle of all and every citizen in our territories, whose right it is to live in peace. It is the commitment of conscience and responsibility in the hearts of millions.

When I put forward this initiative, many asked what is it that I conceived as possible to achieve during this visit and what my expectations were. And as I answer the questions, I announce before you that I have not thought of carrying out this initiative from the precepts of what could be achieved during this visit. And I have come here to deliver a message. I have delivered the message, and may God be my witness.

I repeat with Zachariah: Love, right, and justice. From the holy Koran I quote the following verses: We believe in God and in what has been revealed to us and what was revealed to Abraham, Ishmael, Isaac, Jacob, and the thirteen Jewish tribes. And in the books given to Moses and Jesus and the prophets from their Lord, who made no distinction between them. So we agree. *Salam Aleikum*—Peace be upon you.

Prerequisites for Peace Accords

Jimmy Carter

President Jimmy Carter worked diligently toward peace in the Middle East from the beginning of his term in 1976. He even believed the Soviet Union could function as a powerful partner in the process. It is in the following speech that Carter offers the "good offices" of the United States in helping to broker peace with Israel after Egyptian President Anwar el-Sadat expressed interest in mending relations with Egypt's longtime enemy.

In the speech given at a town meeting forum in Clinton, Massachusetts, Carter outlines specific prerequisites for achieving peace in the region. First, the president insists that Israel's right to exist must be recognized by her neighbors—to exist permanently and in peace. This meant not only recognizing the state, but also opening the borders to commerce and cultural exchange. The second prerequisite is the establishment of permanent borders for Israel. He admitted that this was the most difficult component of the plan. The third requirement for peace is the creation of a Palestinian homeland. This was the first time that the idea of a homeland for Palestinians was supported by the U.S. government. Finally, Carter essentially denies that America's role in the peace process stems from an interest in oil, a criticism often levied against the United States. The speech eventually led to the historic meeting between Israeli Prime Minister Menachem Begin and Egyptian President Anwar el-Sadat at Camp David, Maryland in 1978. Agreement on two accords followed, known as the "Camp David Accords," as

Jimmy Carter, town meeting address, Clinton, Massachusetts, March 16, 1977.

well as the eventual signing of an Egypt-Israel Peace
Treaty in 1979, ending more than four decades of war
between the two nations.

I think all of you know that there has been either war or
potential war in the Middle East for the last 29 years,
ever since Israel became a nation. I think one of the finest
acts of the world nations that's ever occurred was to establish the State of Israel.

So, the first prerequisite of a lasting peace is the recognition of Israel by her neighbors, Israel's right to exist, Israel's
right to exist permanently, Israel's right to exist in peace.
That means that over a period of months or years that the
borders between Israel and Syria, Israel and Lebanon, Israel
and Jordan, Israel and Egypt must be opened up to travel, to
tourism, to cultural exchange, to trade, so that no matter
who the leaders might be in those countries, the people themselves will have formed a mutual understanding and compre-
hension and a sense of a common purpose to avoid the rep-
etitious wars and death that have afflicted that region so
long. That's the first prerequisite of peace.

The second one is very important and very, very difficult;
and that is, the establishment of permanent borders for Israel. The Arab countries say that Israel must withdraw to the
pre-1967 borderlines, Israel says that they must adjust those
lines to some degree to insure their own security. That is a
matter to be negotiated between the Arab countries on the
one side and Israel on the other.

But borders are still a matter of great trouble and a matter of great difficulty, and there are strong differences of
opinion now.

And the third ultimate requirement for peace is to deal
with the Palestinian problem. The Palestinians claim up to
this day, this moment, that Israel has no right to be there,
that the land belongs to the Palestinians, and they've never
yet given up their publicly professed commitment to destroy
Israel. That has to be overcome.

There has to be a homeland provided for the Palestinian

refugees who have suffered for many, many years. And the exact way to solve the Palestinian problem is one that first of all addresses itself right now to the Arab countries and then, secondly, to the Arab countries negotiating with Israel.

Those three major elements have got to be solved before a Middle Eastern solution can be prescribed.

America's Role

I want to emphasize one more time, we offer our good offices. I think it's accurate to say that of all the nations in the world, we are the one that's most trusted, not completely, but most trusted by the Arab countries and also Israel. I guess both sides have some doubt about us. But we'll have to act as kind of a catalyst to bring about their ability to negotiate successfully with one another.

Jimmy Carter

We hope that later on this year, in the latter part of this year, that we might get all of these parties to agree to come together at Geneva, to start talking to one another. They haven't done that yet. And I believe if we can get them to sit down and start talking and negotiating that we have an excellent chance to achieve peace. I can't guarantee that. It's a hope.

I hope that we will all pray that that will come to pass, because what happens in the Middle East in the future might very well cause a major war there which would quickly spread to all the other nations of the world; very possibly it could do that.

Many countries depend completely on oil from the Middle East for their life. We don't. If all oil was cut off to us from the Middle East, we could survive; but Japan imports more than 98 percent of all its energy, and other countries, like in Europe—Germany, Italy, France are also heavily dependent on oil from the Middle East.

So, this is such a crucial area of the world that I will be devoting a major part of my own time on foreign policy between now and next fall trying to provide for a forum within which they can discuss their problems and, hopefully, let them seek out among themselves some permanent solution.

We Have Labored Long for Peace

Menachem Begin

In 1977, Menachem Begin became Israel's prime minister, the first from the moderate Likud Party that he helped create. Previously he founded the Herut Party, which was known for its right wing, strongly nationalistic views and its opposition to evacuating the many territories occupied by Israel in the Six-Day War.

Despite his hawkish, or prowar, background, when Anwar el-Sadat of Egypt expressed interest in traveling to Israel for peace talks, Begin immediately welcomed him to Jerusalem. This was a major step in establishing relations between the antagonistic nations. Israel was still reeling from the Yom Kippur War in 1973, a surprise attack Egypt launched against Israel while they were observing a holy day. Still, after waging several wars with Egypt, Begin became the first Israeli prime minister to meet publicly and officially with an Arab head of state. He negotiated with Sadat at Camp David under the auspices of U.S. president Jimmy Carter. He agreed to give up the Sinai Peninsula, an immense territory filled with Israeli settlements. This effectively ended the four-decade-long antagonism with Egypt, the Arab world's most populous and militarily powerful state.

For their efforts to bring peace to the region, Sadat and Begin were honored with the Nobel Peace Prize in December 1978. During his acceptance speech, excerpted below, Begin calls peace "That human dream. That unshakable faith." He seems dedicated to cooperation and development within the Middle East as he vows to con-

Menachem Begin, statement upon receiving the Nobel Peace Prize, December 10, 1978.

tinue working toward peace with all of Israel's neighbors. Indeed, this was a pivotal moment in the Arab-Israeli conflict and for the world. Many saw it as a beginning, a sign of hope for permanent peace. However, in 1981, Begin's partner in peace, Egypt's Sadat, was assassinated. Then in 1982, Israel launched a war in Lebanon in response to Palestinian attacks launched from Lebanese territory. The atmosphere of peace in the region quickly disintegrated.

I have come from the land of Israel. The land of Zion and Jerusalem. And here I stand in humility and with pride as a son of the Jewish people, as one of the generation of the Holocaust and the redemption.

The ancient Jewish people gave the world the vision of eternal peace, of universal disarmament, of abolishing the teaching and learning of war. Two prophets, Yeshayahu ben Amotz and Micha Hamorashti, having foreseen the spiritual unity of man under God—with His word coming forth from Jerusalem—gave the nations of the world the following vision expressed in identical terms:

> And they shall beat their swords into ploughshares and their spears into pruning hooks, nation shall not lift up sword against nation, neither shall they learn war any more.

A Belief in Providence

We mortals who believe in Divine Providence when recalling these sacred prophecies, ask ourselves not whether, but when, is this vision going to become reality. We remember the past. Even in this century alone—and we know, we look around—we see millions of men of all nations under arms. Intercontinental missiles deposited in the bowels of the earth or lying on the beds of the oceans can destroy man and everything he has built.

Not in Alfred Nobel's time, but in our own era, has mankind become capable of destroying itself and returning the earth to *tohu vavohu*. Under such circumstances, should we, can we, keep our faith in an eternal peace that will one day reign over mankind? Yes. We should and we can. Perhaps that very capability of total destruction of our little planet—achieved for the first time in the annals of mankind—will one day, God willing, become the origin, the cause and the prime mover for the elimination of all instruments of destruction from the face of the earth and ultimate peace, prayed for and yearned for by previous generations, will become a portion of all nations, despite the tragedies and disappointments of the past. We must never forsake that vision. That human dream. That unshakable faith.

What Peace Will Bring

Peace is the beauty of life, it is sunshine, it is the smile of a child, the love of a mother, the joy of a father, the togetherness of a family. It is the advancement of man, the victory of a just cause, the triumph of truth. Peace is all of these and more.

And so reborn Israel always strove for peace. Yearned for it. Made endless endeavors to achieve it.

My colleagues and I have gone in the footsteps of our predecessors since the very first day we were called by our people to care for their future. We went any place. We looked for any avenue. We made any effort to bring about negotiations between Israel and its neighbors. Negotiations without which peace remains an abstract desire.

We have labored long and hard to turn it into a reality—because of the blessings it holds for ourselves, for our neighbors. The world. In peace, the Middle East, the ancient cradle of civilization, will become invigorated and transformed. Throughout its lands there will be freedom of movement of people, of ideas, of goods, and cooperation and development in agriculture will make the deserts blossom. Industry will bring the promise of a better life. Sources of water will be developed and the almost year-long sunshine will yet be harnessed for the common needs of all the nations. Yes, indeed, the Middle East, standing at the crossroads of the world, will become a peaceful center of international communication between East and West, North and South—a center of human advancement in every sphere of creative endeavor. This and more is what peace will bring to our region.

Chapter FOUR

GREAT
SPEECHES
IN
HISTORY

The First Intifada and a Renewed Hope

The Future of Jordan Is Linked to the Future of Palestine

King Hussein I

King Hussein I was the Middle East's longest ruling leader, reigning as monarch for forty-six years. He joined his neighboring Arab nations against Israel in the Six-Day War of 1967. In the 1970s, however, he enjoyed close relations with the West as he fought against Palestine Liberation Organization (PLO) guerillas and threats from Syria. In 1985 Hussein mended relations with the PLO, ending the rift that existed since Jordan's annexation of Palestinian lands in the 1948 war.

While often at odds with Yasser Arafat and PLO leadership, in this speech to the Jordanian congress in 1991, Hussein stresses a partnership with Palestinians in Jordan and the necessity to begin a peaceful dialogue with Israel. On one level, this speech explains Hussein's decision in 1988 to relinquish control over Palestine land and Palestinian concerns to the PLO, treating them not as subjects but agents in their own destiny. He notes the new relationship between the United States and the Soviet Union, from adversaries to allies in the peace process. He also examines the current unrest in the Middle East, the lack of a clear power broker amid the Arab countries, and the impact of the 1991 Gulf War in the region. As one of the most respected leaders in the region, Hussein's speech carried significant weight in the Arab community.

King Hussein I, address to the Jordanian National Congress, October 12, 1991.

He convinced Jordanians it was in their national interest to support relations with Israel. In the next two years Israel made great strides with the PLO in the Oslo Accords, and in 1994 Jordan signed a definitive peace agreement with Israel's Prime Minister Yitzak Rabin, ending nearly a half century of war and conflict.

Modern Jordan was founded to protect this land and its people. Throughout the years the region has witnessed certain developments which placed Jordan on the longest borders and in a sacred position, making it the avant-garde of its Arab nation. Recently, events have accelerated in a manner that have overtaken our national agenda which was based on formulating a National Charter, and which has been accomplished. The next phase was to translate the principles of this National Charter into reality and in the form of political pluralism and political parties, whose Pan-Arab and universal outlook emanate from the Jordanian homeland and its message, functioning in conformity with the provisions of the constitution and the principles of the National Charter. Pursuant to that, general parliamentary elections based on political pluralism were to be held.

A Critical Time for Jordan

Were it not for those events which took us by surprise, we would have carried out our national agenda as scheduled, and there would have been no need to hold this meeting to brief, through you, our people about an issue that will constitute, as I expect, a watershed between uncertainty and clarity of vision, between evading responsibility and shouldering it, and between burying one's head in the sand and standing up to reality by confronting challenges with courage, determination and faith.

Thus, I believe it is my duty to speak to you at this critical juncture and at a decisive turning point upon which our whole existence, progress and regional and international relations depend.

That turning point is the peace conference on the Middle East and the fruits it might yield should it succeed, in the form of a new reality that would put an end to the state of fragmentation, uncertainty and waste of time, and usher in a new era of hope, relief and progress. This is the true meaning of a just and lasting peace which we have been striving and will continue to strive to achieve. I believe it does not surprise you that I speak about peace, or about our earnest efforts to attain peace, to preach its preeminence within our hopes, to emphasize its importance for us to continue our progress and pursue our march as a state. Peace is essential to us in leading a normal life which is the legitimate right of every individual, in order to dream, plan for oneself, and for the future of one's family, to raise one's standard of living away from fear, worry and confusion. It is also the legitimate right of each nation in order to develop and progress free from threat and preventing the exhaustion of the country's capabilities and resources. We have been discussing the peace issue for a long time. We have made it a symbol for a better life for future generations. In the light of the developments of the Palestinian problem with all the pain, complications and sacrifices that entailed to our steadfast homeland, peace has become a national objective that we have striven to attain, and a political strategic foundation upon which to proceed.

On this basis, we have played a central role at both the Arab and international levels. For over a quarter of a century we were amongst the first to initiate efforts and contribute toward resolving the Palestinian problem and the establishment of a just and lasting peace in the Middle East.

Consequently we have, since 1967, responded positively to every peace initiative based on international legitimacy. We welcomed President Bush's speech to the United States Congress on the 6th of March in which he declared his determination to end the Arab-Israeli conflict and to resolve the Palestinian problem on the basis of United Nations Security Council Resolutions 242 and 338 and the principle of land for peace, as well as the restoration of the legitimate political rights of the Palestinian people and guaranteeing security to all countries of the region.

In fact, we have consistently reaffirmed in every political

statement we made our adherence to a just and comprehensive peace and the need to implement United Nations Security Council Resolutions 242 and 338 as the basis for any peaceful settlement of this conflict. Even when we and the whole world were preoccupied with the Gulf crisis, the case of peace never escaped our attention. We expressed this through our insistence that the International Community should deal with Israel's occupation of Arab land with the same measures with which it dealt with Iraq's occupation of Kuwait [during the Gulf War]. We called earnestly for the linking between resolving both conflicts on the same basis of international legitimacy. As a result of many considerations and serious international changes, the time has now come when a serious attempt to resolve the Arab-Israeli conflict and to establish peace is being made through the convening of a Conference. What is our position? What are we to do?

Why Jordan Should Get Involved

One might ask: Why should we go to the peace conference while the Israeli leadership constantly insists that it will not give one inch of the occupied territories? The answer to this is: Our cause is not only between us and Israel but also between the world and Israel. It is between the supremacy of international law in strengthening world peace and the flouting of it. The whole world rejects what Israel's leadership is saying because it contravenes international legitimacy. Indeed, a relatively growing segment of Israelis are not too far from this world view. The Israeli leadership has in the past adopted this view regarding the settlements in the Sinai, when it kept insisting on not dismantling those settlements. However, the Israeli government then had to change its position as a result of the negotiations and international pressure it found itself under to reach peace with Egypt which had adhered to the principle of international legitimacy.

Besides, let us assume that Israel will adopt a rigid position in the negotiations with the purpose of preserving the status quo to its advantage. This will make it clear to the world that Israel is the enemy of peace and stability in the region contrary to what it has been claiming, because it is clear that the basis for resolving the conflict should be international legitimacy and the principle of land for peace. In this case, Israel will stand to lose more than us. In fact our losses will be far greater if we do not participate than if we do and fail in the negotiations. Because just peace would touch every aspect of our lives, it necessitates our serious response to every serious attempt to achieve it. Hence, to make efforts trying to achieve it is a national duty. To run away from it is letting our nation down irrespective of any cosmetic justification.

Also one might say: Since only a small patch of Jordanian territory is occupied by Israel what is in the conference for us?

The answer to this is: Since when can we separate Jordan's future from the reality and future of the Palestinian problem? And since when is diplomacy conducted without any consideration of geographic proximity and demographic links? Didn't our political history and our socio-economic conditions take shape as a consequence of the Palestinian problem and how it developed? Didn't Jordan receive three huge waves of displaced Palestinians until now? Didn't this cause an imbalance in the equation of resources and people which in turn led to the current socio-economic hardships we now face? Nevertheless, Jordanians should be proud that had their country not been established on this land, nothing would have been left to discuss now. And that had it not been for their sacrifices and struggle throughout the course of the Palestinian problem there would not have been a West Bank left for us to retrieve for its rightful owners on the basis of Security Council resolutions; that had it not been for the unity of Jordan and the West Bank, that included Arab Jerusalem which we saved in 1948, we would not have the cause of Jerusalem, especially since all other Arab states stood with the rest of the world in favor of the internationalization of the Holy City except for Pakistan, and Britain who were bound to Jordan by a treaty. Jordanians, irrespective of their roots, should be proud that, together, they have withstood the consequences of the tragedy which fell upon Palestine and its people.

The answer is also: The conference is a Peace Conference. In other words, the retrieving of territory would be one and

not all of its consequences. For there is also the issue of regional security and peace between the countries of the region
as well as the issue of the environment, water and economic
development. These issues require cooperation and collective
agreements. Jordan, which is at the center of the east Mediterranean Region, cannot disassociate itself from the efforts
aimed at resolving those issues and not be a part in the agreements that could be reached. These issues concern Jordan, its
future and its regional role, I doubt that any of our people
would expect us to be so naive as to choose to isolate ourselves, be forgotten and wither away. I am sure that you are
aware that this particular phase of the world's history is one
of interdependence between peoples and nations. Thus, we
must be involved in the drive for peace because it concerns
our present and future and has an impact on our continuity.
Otherwise the outcome, God forbid, will be ominous dangers.

Brothers and Sisters, Members of the Jordanian National
Congress, God said in His Holy Book:

> *"For the covenants of security and safeguard enjoyed by*
> *the Quraysh, their covenants covering journeys by winter*
> *and summer, let them adore the Lord of this House, who*
> *provides them with food against hunger, and with security*
> *against fear of danger."*

An introspective reading of this divine Sura reveals that
God in His wisdom has defined for any caretaker his responsibilities toward his followers, for all times and places,
in two essential ways: That of providing them with food
against hunger, and securing against fear of danger.
Certainly, the contemporary interpretation of preventing
hunger cannot mean the opening of poorhouses or the distri-
bution of free meals. Indeed, it means the creation of job opportunities through utilizing the state's resources, educating
and training its citizens to participate in developing all sectors of society. As far as securing them against fear of danger
is concerned, it also has many definitions, ranging from the
respect and protection of human rights and freedoms, to ensuring material and social security for the individual citizen,
and protecting the state's stability and security. This is the
leadership's foremost responsibility. In all honesty, I tell you

that it has become increasingly difficult to shoulder these responsibilities under the current conditions. Indeed, it has become a great challenge to do so, a challenge which is obvious to all those who are aware of Jordan's difficult financial, economic and social conditions. Jordan is practically under siege; Jordan has limited resources; Jordan has one of the highest population growth rates; in short, Jordan has both unemployment and hunger.

On the other hand, Jordan is a country whose people have pride and dignity and are imbued with perseverance, determination and loyalty. Our participation in the Peace Conference is not, therefore, aimed at achieving peace in its narrow sense or at any price. We will participate out of a sense of duty to ensure, in the first place, security and prosperity for our people, and out of determination to adhere to international legitimacy. We will participate to restore our rights, honoring our loyalty to our Jerusalem and our commitment to stand beside the Palestinian people and to help them put an end to their tragedy by regaining their sovereignty on their soil; to support them to obtain their legitimate rights so that they can live like other people, secure in their homeland seeking their prosperity.

Peace which results from negotiations is permanent because it is the outcome of mutual understanding and accommodation between the parties to the conflict, but without sacrificing rights or deviating from the principle of international legitimacy. For peace to be permanent it must be balanced and not governed by a disparity between the materially strong and weak. It must be founded on the basis of right and justice and the common good of those who conclude it. This will, therefore, insure that future generations will reap its benefits, and will, protect it. Hence, the principle of the inadmissibility of the acquisition of territory by war stipulated in the Charter of the United Nations cannot be forfeited or ignored. It is the genesis of United Nations Security Council Resolution 242 which applies to Arab Jerusalem as well as the West Bank, the Gaza Strip and the Syrian Golan Heights. This Resolution means the complete withdrawal of all Israeli forces from the Arab occupied territories including Arab Jerusalem, exactly as was understood in the Egyptian peace treaty when Israel withdrew from the Sinai which it occupied as a result of the same war. This also means that the settlements are illegal and that to continue with this policy is rendering the principle of land for peace void of its content. This policy would then constitute an obstacle to the peace process which must be removed. . . .

Developments That Affect the Peace Process

First, let me remind you of a fact I previously made reference to, namely that no observer closely scrutinizing the graph line of the Palestinian issue can fail to notice its steady decline. To be sure, what could have been achieved out of any peace opportunity has always proved to be less than that offered by the previous one. This, indeed, has been the trend since the thirties despite the justice of the issue. If there is any significance to this it can only mean that our grasp, as Arabs and Palestinians, of the regional and international situation at every peace opportunity had always fallen short of what was required. Indeed, we have failed to deal with the events within the framework of what is possible and reasonable and have, consequently, lost one opportunity after another. This led to a situation whereby sixty-five percent of the West Bank territories have been confiscated by Israel, and where the plight of the Palestinian people today is one best described as dispersion and uncertainty in the Diaspora and increased suffering and hardship in the occupied territories.

Second, the present Israeli leadership feels itself to be the only beneficiary from the continuation of the status quo, i.e. the state of no-war no-peace—a situation Israel is exploiting to bring about changes on the ground.

There are three facts that encourage Israel to cling to this status quo, facts which we are familiar with and concerned about on a daily basis:

1. The continuous flow of Soviet Jews into Israel by the tens of thousands.

2. The establishment of new settlements.

3. Raising funds from outside sources in order to absorb these immigrants.

Such facts, as plainly evident, are of a dynamic nature and not simply transient. Only a just peace based on international legitimacy can put an end to this ever growing evil, leading to the seizure of territories and to the dispersion of the Palestinians by uprooting and expelling them.

Third, the collapse of communism and its alliance and the consequent breakdown of the international balance of power, led not only to the end of the Cold War and a World Order based essentially on bipolarity, but also to a peace-oriented world, nuclear disarmament, reduction in armed forces, elimination of weapons of mass destruction, the settlement of all regional conflicts, and the protection of the world environment.

Regarding the effect of this state of affairs on the Middle East, the Soviet Union has shifted from the position of a rival to that of partner of the United States in the proposed peace process. This shift was effected by a shared concept of the two superpowers of a new World Order succeeding the Cold War era. At the same time, the Soviet Union has ceased to be a source of threat to Western, and particularly American, interests in the region—a fact that has deprived Israel of its most significant asset, namely, being the United States strategic ally in confronting the Soviet Union.

Fourth, the collapse of the Arab order, the disequilibrium in the Middle East balance of power, the new alliances, and the drifting elusively toward the nation-states concerns as a consequence of the Gulf crisis. This has left an immediate impact on the Arab outlook regarding the Palestinian issue, as well as on the security considerations of each Arab country.

Fifth, Jordanians and Palestinians are besieged and they are the parties directly and adversely affected by the continuation of the status quo of the Arab-Israeli conflict.

Sixth, the increased American interest in post-Gulf War stability in the Middle East—a stability based on the settlement of conflicts and the treatment of their root causes, and not one merely based on the containment and management of crises as has been the case until quite recently. This development, within the context of establishing and consolidating stability, emanated from two factors:

I. The end of the Cold War period and the beginning of

a new phase in which all indications show that competition will essentially be economic and scientific but not military as was the case in the past.

II. The consequences of the Gulf War and the emphasis it laid on the need to provide stability not only in the oil states but in the neighboring ones too. The roots of the conflicts in these neighboring countries are diverse: some are political, some economic, others racial and sectarian. In any event, the Arab-Israeli conflict and the Palestinian issue is the most predominant.

All these events and developments, and the regional and international relations they have entailed, subsequently brought about one essential outcome, namely the renewal of efforts in an attempt to arrive at a peaceful settlement of the Arab-Israeli conflict, hence the US/Soviet initiative to convene a Middle East peace conference. Thus, the Arabs and the rest of the world meet in their mutual desire and interests to find a peaceful solution to the Arab-Israeli conflict.

The Arab Stance

Before discussing this convergence, its elements and its potential, let me outline to you the development of the Arab stance vis-a-vis peace with Israel in terms of the sequence of events that commenced on November 1967, when two Arab states, of those that had engaged in war with Israel, accepted United Nations Security Council Resolution 242 calling for peace on the basis of the inadmissibility of the acquisition of territory by war. The two states were Jordan and Egypt. Following the October 1973 War United Nations Security Council Resolution 338 was adopted. One of the paragraphs of this Resolution provided for measures pertaining to the implementation of Resolution 242—a provision that was accepted by Syria, thereby joining Jordan and Egypt. In 1979 Egypt concluded a peace treaty with Israel. At the Fez Summit Conference in 1982, Arab leaders including the PLO, unanimously agreed to accept a peaceful settlement of the Arab-Israeli conflict and to resolve the Palestinian issue. In 1988, the 19th session of the Palestinian National Council declared a Palestinian peace initiative based on the existence of two states on the territories of Palestine—one Israeli and one Palestinian. The PLO accepted United Nations Security Council Resolutions 242 and 338. . . .

An End to Destruction

Brothers and Sisters,

We are at a crossroads made by national and global realities which touch every Jordanian here and every Palestinian in the occupied territories and in the Diaspora [outside those territories].

These realities affect our present and future and we have a bearing on our national life and how to deal with the challenges beginning with unemployment and leading to our national identity and our national security. These realities demand the historic decision of participating in the Peace Conference. This conference, if it succeeds, will enable us to transform these realities into positive forces that will take us from despair to hope, from confrontation and four decades of suffering, anxiety and pain that accompanied it, and which left an imprint on our lives, to peace and its promise of security, stability, opportunities and prosperity for all; from the no-war no-peace situation and the continuation of the status quo with its real dangers, to a condition of certainty and ease which will enhance the creativity and hopes of the younger generation.

Consequently, we in Jordan, while being fully aware of the real situation and the global and regional realities, and in light of the great sufferings of the Palestinians in the occupied territories and the oppressive policies that they have been subjected to, as well as the threat to their presence and existence on their soil as a result of immigration and settlements, and because of the direct effects this will have on Jordan, will therefore participate in the Peace Conference. We will participate in order to protect ourselves and to safeguard our country and our people, to enable us to lead a normal life, and in order to halt the depletion of our resources and energies. This will allow us to maintain support for the struggling Palestinian people who have endured more than what can be described.

In short, this is our decision which we make for the sake

of a just peace which will renew hope in ourselves and put an end to the status quo which, if it is maintained, will continue to gnaw at us bit by bit until it is too late.

Let us awake and put an end to self-destruction in our minds and our beings. Let us put an end to the sweeping tendencies of outbidding each other and to illusions. Let us heed God, for our nation, our children, our present and our future. Let us shoulder our responsibilities and not seek escapism under the guise of leaving it to future generations. Let us remember that the majority of Jordanians and Palestinians cannot afford the luxury of betting on the unknown.

Let me disclose this to you—as you know, I am on the threshold of my autumn years of shouldering responsibility. I am now in the fortieth year on the throne and in the thirty-ninth year since I assumed my constitutional powers. Recently, a question has been weighing heavily on me: should I give in to the call within me to rest, which I badly need, or should I continue to maintain the trust you have placed with me? I contemplated the question and thought of the difficult period our country is going through. I concluded that to think of doing so now is no more than an escape from duty. I then decided to continue to shoulder my responsibilities in spite of the hardships involved in the hope that, with God's help, we pass through this difficult phase into a better one for you, my brothers and sisters, sons and daughters. I praise God, whom I fear none but Him. I thank Him who has guided me to be amongst those who only seek His satisfaction, serving their nations and living with a clear conscience, so that the judgment of future generations will be for them, not against them.

Depending on God and His guidance, we beseech the Almighty to help us to shoulder this historic responsibility through which we seek His satisfaction and the well-being of our people and nation.

May God's peace and blessings be with you.

Israel Continues to Challenge the International Community

H.E. Gaafar Allagany

Saudi Arabia has consistently held a pivotal position in the Middle East, both culturally and religiously. It contains both Mecca and Medina, the centers of the Islamic faith. Economically, it possesses the largest oil reserves on the planet. Politically and militarily, its conservative monarchy has historically played a ready ally to Western powers.

In December 1992, H.E. Gaafar Allagany, ambassdor to the United Nations, spoke to the General Assembly in an effort to voice Arab sentiment regarding the Palestinian uprising in the contested areas of Israel.

In this speech, it is clear that Saudi Arabia, and the Arab community in general, consider Israel the great usurper of land. He concentrates most of his speech in condemning immigration into Israel and the state's "false dictum . . . 'a land without a people, for a people without a land.'" Among his demands for Israel is compliance with the many UN resolutions which call for a complete withdrawal from all Arab territories occupied since 1967, especially Jerusalem, and the withdrawal of Israeli forces from Southern Lebanon. A key negotiating factor in his speech is Saudi Arabia's promise of non-proliferation of nuclear weapons, a treaty that will extend to neighboring Arab states, and he hopes, Israel as well.

H.E. Gaafar Allagany, statement before the United Nations General Assembly, December 4, 1992.

Mr. President:
The Middle East is at the forefront of the regions which occupy the attention of the international community and take a large share of international efforts.

A quick survey of the situation in the Middle East shows that it threatens not only the security and stability of the region, but also international peace and security. Israel occupied large portions of Arab lands during the 1967 war, most of which are still under its control 25 years later. Until now, peace has not been achieved in the region, and the Palestinians are not one step closer to achieving their national rights, including their right to self-determination.

Since then, Israel continued to challenge the international community by planning and executing policies that aim at usurping these lands, while continuing at the same time to dispossess the Palestinians of their lands. Israel worked at shrinking the Palestinian population in the occupied territories and at converting the land into a colony. Israel continued with its original objective, which is to tighten its control of the occupied territories and suppress any Arab resistance in them.

Israeli Disregard for UN Resolutions

The Fourth Geneva Convention prohibits, in Article 47, the annexation of lands occupied by military force. The United Nations passed resolutions condemning these Israeli policies in East Jerusalem and other Arab towns and cities. Article 49 of the same convention prohibits the transfer or expulsion of the original population in the areas they live or outside their territories, no matter what the causes or reasons. Yet, we still see the Palestinians being expelled from their lands. The same article prohibits the occupying authorities from transferring their citizens to the lands they occupy. Yet, Israel continues to increase the number of settlements, which the reports before us say constitute more than 60 per cent of the West Bank and Gaza that were appropriated by military orders from 1967 until 1992; 230,000 Israelis have been settled in 212 settlements in the occupied Palestinian lands, including the holy city of Jerusalem. The same situation is in the Syrian Arab Golan where the occupying authority endeavors to change its demographic character by increasing the number of settlements.

Israeli estimates say that Israel will receive more than 100,000 new settlers by the end of this year, and that the new settlers will reach 2 million in the Golan during the next five years. Former Israeli Prime Minister Yitzhak Shamir alluded to this plan when he said "large scale immigration will require a greater Israel." At present, there are only five Arab villages out of the original 110 which were in existence before the occupation. Forty-five Israeli settlements are built on the ruins of Syrian Arab villages in the Golan. Israel has expelled 93 percent of the Golan population in order to realize its false dictum in the Arab Syrian lands, "a land without a people, for a people without a land." Israel continues to execute its plans to change the historical, cultural, social and economic characteristics of the occupied territories on which it imposed its administration, its laws, and its identity in order to erase the Arab identity of the occupied Golan, in contradiction to Security Council Resolution 497 (1981) and other related United Nations resolutions.

The nature of the Israeli policies has become clear for the international community; from the principle of invasion for the purpose of occupation, to the principle of deprivation from natural and human resources and the imposition of mass economic punishment, Israel takes measures like brutal force, demolition of houses, pulling out trees as well as other oppressive measures. The objective is the same, which is the gradual annexation of occupied Arab lands.

Israel did not stop with the lands occupied in 1967. It invaded another Arab country, Lebanon, and it still occupies the southern portion. From time to time, it bombards the villages and towns in southern Lebanon and western Bekaa valley, which results in innocent casualties and great material losses. Israel's continued deplorable aggression against Lebanon aims at preempting the implementation of United Nations resolutions, particularly Security Council Resolution 425, which requires Israel to withdraw from southern Lebanon. In this regard, we have to affirm that Israel must be committed to complete and unconditional implementation of Security Council Resolution 425 so that the Lebanese government will be able to exercise its legitimate authority over all Lebanese soil. I have to stress here that the Lebanese government has achieved great progress in its efforts to implement the Taif Agreement by taking all necessary political and constitutional measures. The international community must continue to support these Lebanese efforts and participate in the reconstruction of Lebanon. In this connection, the Kingdom of Saudi Arabia appeals to the international community to work towards the establishment of an international fund for the reconstruction of Lebanon.

Saudi Arabia's Contribution to Peace

The time has come for the Middle East region to receive its share of security, peace, and tranquility, and for all energies to be directed towards stability and development. The Arab countries have asserted their sincere intentions to establish permanent and just peace in the Middle East. They have proven this by participating in the peace negotiations which are co-hosted by the United States and the Russian Federation. The Kingdom of Saudi Arabia has given its full support to the peace process in the Middle East. It believes that peace requires the elimination of the dangers of weapons of mass destruction in the Middle East. It is imperative to convince all the countries in the region without exception to desist from producing, stockpiling, or acquiring any such weapons. In fact, the Kingdom of Saudi Arabia and all other Arab states have implemented, by word and deed, the treaty for the non-proliferation of nuclear weapons. It is now imperative that all countries in the region, including Israel, must become parties to this treaty in order to achieve a balance that guarantees security, peace and stability to all.

The Kingdom of Saudi Arabia believes in finding a just solution to the situation in the Middle East. It also believes that no real peace will be achieved in the Middle East unless a permanent and just solution to the Palestinian issue is found, and unless there is a complete withdrawal of Israel from all Arab territories occupied since the 1967 war, foremost of which is the holy city of Jerusalem, which is an integral part of the occupied territories, and unless Israel withdraws from Southern Lebanon. The success of the current peace process in the Middle East clearly depends on Israel's serious implementation of Security Council Resolutions 242 and 338 and all other related United Nations resolutions.

The time has come for this region to receive its share of security, peace and stability, and for all its resources to be devoted to the prosperity of its peoples. The Middle East region can offer a decent living for all who live there and can become an oasis of progress and ingenuity, thus returning to what it once used to be, a fountain of human civilization.

Thank you, Mr. President.

The Palestinian Peace Initiative

Yasser Arafat

In the late 1980s, Palestinians living in the West Bank and Gaza took to the streets, armed with little more than rocks and sticks, to fight Israeli occupation of those lands. The uprising was known as the first intifida. In 1988, soon after the revolt began, Palestine Liberation Organization (PLO) leader Yasser Arafat spoke before the United Nation's General Assembly, asking for UN protection and assistance against Israel's military response to the uprising. Arafat makes it quite clear that the Palestinians have waited long enough for their homeland, a UN promise dating back to 1948.

With UN pressure, Israel and Palestinian authorities opened peace talks. An era of fruitful negotiations seemed at hand. In the next five years, Israel would go from making open war against Palestinians in Gaza and the West Bank to peace treaties with Jordan, establishing a dialogue with Syria, and signing major accords with Arafat and the PLO.

A little more than a decade later, however, peace talks stalled and Israel was still in control of Palestine. Perhaps recalling the successful bargaining influence of the first Palestinian uprisings, Arafat called for a second intifada to protest the political inertia that doomed Palestinian independence.

Yasser Arafat, address before the United Nations General Assembly, Geneva, December 1988.

Mr. President, Honorable Members:
Fourteen Years ago on 13 November 1974, I received a gracious invitation from you to expound the problem of our Palestinian people before this dignified assembly. Here I am returning to you after all these eventful years to see now peoples taking their places in your midst, crowning thereby their victories in the battles for freedom and independence. To the representatives of these peoples, I extend the warm congratulations of our own. Let it be known that I return to you with a stronger voice, a firmer determination and a greater coincidence to reiterate my conviction that our struggle will bear fruit and that the State of Palestine, which we proclaimed at our Palestine National Council, will take its place among you to join [hands with] you in consolidating the charter of this organization and the Universal Declaration of Human Rights, in putting an end to the tragedies afflicting humanity, and in upholding the principles of right, justice, peace, and freedom for all.

Fourteen years ago, when you told us in the General Assembly hall-"Yes to Palestine and the people Palestine, yes to the Palestine Liberation Organization, yes to the inalienable national rights of the people of Palestine," a few imagined that your resolutions would carry little weight, failing to realize that these resolutions were among the springs that watered the olive branch I carried that day. Since then, we have watered it with blood, tears, and sweat, and it has turned into a tree with roots entrenched in the ground, and a stem reaching for the sky promising to bear the fruits of victory over coercion, injustice, and occupation.

You gave us hope that freedom and justice would triumph and we gave you a generation of our people that has dedicated its life to the realization of that dream. It is the generation of the blessed *intifadah*, which today is wielding the homeland's stones to defend the honor of this homeland and be worthy of belonging to a people thirsting for freedom and independence. . .

I said in concluding my address in our first encounter that as chairman of the Palestine Liberation Organization and leader of the Palestine revolution, I reaffirm that we do not wish to see a drop of Jewish or Arab blood shed, that we do not want the continuation of the fighting for one extra minute. I appealed to you then to spare us all these ordeals and sufferings and to speed up work on the foundations of a just peace based on securing the rights, hopes, and aspirations of our people and the equal rights of all peoples.

I said that I was calling upon you to stand by the struggle of our people to exercise its right to self-determination and to enable our people to return from the exile into which it was driven at gunpoint. I solicited your help to end this injustice to which successive generations of our people have been subjected over several decades so that they can live free and sovereign on their soil and in their homeland, enjoying all their national and human rights. The last thing I said from this rostrum, was that war breaks out from Palestine and that peace starts in Palestine.

The dream we entertained at the time was to establish a democratic State of Palestine in which Muslims, Christians, and Jews would live with equal rights and obligations as one unified community, like other peoples in this contemporary world.

We were shocked to hear Israeli officialdom interpret this Palestinian dream—inspired by the spiritual heritage that illuminated Palestine and the civilizational and humanitarian values calling for coexistence in a free democratic society—as a scheme to destroy and obliterate their entity.

The PLO Supports Peace

Mr. President:

We had to draw the necessary conclusion regarding the gap between this reality and the dream. We set out in the Palestine Liberation Organization to look for realistic and attainable formulas that would settle the issue on the basis of possible, rather than absolute, justice while securing the rights of our people to freedom, sovereignty, and independence; ensuring for everyone peace, security, and stability; and sparing Palestine and the Middle East wars and battles that have been going on for forty years.

Didn't we, Mr. President, take the initiative of relying on the charter and resolutions of the United Nations, the Declaration of Human Rights, and international legitimacy as the basis for the settlement of the Arab-Israeli conflict?

Did we not welcome the [U.S. and Soviet-backed] Vance-Gromyko communique of 1977 as a move that could form the basis of a proposed solution to this conflict? Did we not agree to participate in the Geneva conference on the basis of the American-Egyptian statement of 1977 to push forward the prospects of a settlement and peace in the region? Did we not endorse the Arab peace plan in Fez in 1982 and later the call for an international peace conference under the auspices of the United Nations and in keeping with its resolutions? Did we not underwrite the Brezhnev plan for peace in the Middle East? Did we not welcome and support the Venice declaration by the European Community as the basis for a just peace in the area? Did we not welcome and support the joint initiative of presidents Gorbachev [of Russia] and Mitterrand [of France] on a preparatory committee for the international conference? Did we not welcome scores of political statements and initiatives put forward by African, Islamic, non-aligned, socialist, European, and other groups and states for the purpose of finding a peaceful settlement based on the principles of international legitimacy?

What has been the attitude of Israel on all this, even though not a single one of the aforementioned initiatives or plans or communiques lacks political balance or overlooks the claims and interests of the parties to the Arab-Israeli conflict?

Israel's response to all this has been the escalation of its settlement and annexation schemes; the fanning of the flames of conflict with more destruction, devastation, and bloodshed; and the expansion of the confrontation fronts to include brotherly Lebanon, which was invaded by the occupation troops in 1982, an invasion punctuated with slaughters and massacres perpetrated against the Lebanese and Palestinian peoples, including the Sabra and Shatila massacres. Until this moment, Israel continues to occupy parts of south Lebanon, and Lebanon faces daily raids as well as air, sea, and land attacks on its cities and villages and our camps in the south.

It is painful and regrettable that the American government alone should continue to back these aggressive and expansionist schemes as well as Israel's continued occupation of Palestinian and Arab territories, its crimes, and its iron-fist policy against our children and women. It is painful and regrettable, too, that the American government should continue refusing to recognize the right of six million Palestinians to self-determination, a right which is sacred to the American people and other peoples on this planet.

I remind them, of the position of President [Woodrow] Wilson, author of the two universal principles of international relations, i.e., the inadmissibility of the acquisition of territory by force and the right of peoples to self-determination. I remind them, too, that when the Palestinian people were consulted by the King-Crane Commission in 1919, they chose the United States as the mandatory power. Circumstances having prevented that, the mandate was given to Britain. My question to the American people is this: Is it fair that the Palestinian people should be deprived of what President Wilson prescribed?

The successive American administrations realize that the only birth certificate for the establishment of the State of Israel is Resolution 181, approved by the General Assembly on 29 November 1947 and endorsed at the time by the United States and the Soviet Union. It provides for the establishment of two states in Palestine, one Palestinian Arab and one Jewish.

How then does the American government explain its position which acknowledges and recognizes the half of the resolution that pertains to Israel and rejects the half pertaining to the Palestinian state? How does the United States government explain its lack of commitment to the execution of a resolution that it has endorsed on more than one occasion in your esteemed assembly, i.e., (UNGA) Resolution 194, which provides for the right of the Palestinians to return to the homes and properties from which they were evicted and for compensation for those wishing not to exercise this right?

The United States government knows that neither the U.S. nor anyone else has the right to apportion international legitimacy and fragment the provisions of international law.

A Democratic Revolution

Mr. President:
The uninterrupted struggle of our people for its rights has

been going on for several decades during which it has offered hundreds of thousands of martyrs and wounded and endured all kinds of tragedies. On the contrary, its adherence to its Palestinian homeland and national identity has grown stronger. . . .

I take pride, Mr. President, in being one of the sons of these population [sic], whose men, women, and children are writing with their blood an outstanding epic of national resistance and who are performing legendary miracles daily to sustain their *intifadah* and make it grow until it can impose its will and prove that fight can prevail over might. We salute with deep pride our people of the *intifadah* as the authors of a unique democratic revolutionary experiment.

Theirs is the faith that could not be crushed by Israel's military machine; that could not be killed by any kind of ammunition; that could not be shaken by the burial of people alive, the breaking of bones, the inducement of miscarriages, or the usurpation of water resources; and that could not be deterred by detention, internment, exile, deportation, collective punishment, the demolition of homes, the closure of universities, schools, trade unions, associations, institutions, and newspapers; or the laying of siege to camps, villages, and towns. Those brutal reprisals have only served to strengthen that faith, spreading it to every household and giving it roots in every inch of our national soil.

A people with such a heritage and such a history is invincible. All the forces of tyranny and terror cannot sway its deep-rooted faith in its right to its homeland and in such values as justice, peace, love, coexistence, and tolerance. The rifle of the revolutionary has protected us from liquidation and the destruction of our national identity in the arenas of hot confrontation. We are fully confident of our ability to protect our green (olive) branch in the arenas of political confrontation.

The worldwide embrace of our just cause, pressing for the realization of peace based on justice, demonstrates clearly that the world has unequivocally identified the predator and the prey, the aggressor and the victim, the struggler for freedom and peace and the terrorist. The day-to-day practices of the occupation army and the gangs of fanatic armed settlers against our people, women and children, have unveiled the ugly face of Israeli occupation and exposed its true aggressive nature.

Distinguishing Between Israelis and Israel's Government

This growing worldwide awareness, has reached Jewish groups within Israel itself and outside. Their eyes have been opened to the reality of the problem and the essence of the conflict, particularly since they have witnessed the inhuman, day-to-day Israeli practices that undermine the tolerant spirit of Judaism itself.

It has become difficult, if not impossible, for a Jew to reject racial persecution and uphold freedom and human rights while remaining silent about Israel's crimes against Palestinian human rights, the Palestinian people, and the Palestinian homeland, particularly the ugly day-to-day practices of the occupier's gangs of settlers.

We distinguish, Mr. President, between the Jewish citizen whom the Israeli ruling circles have continuously sought to disinform and mislead and the practices of the leaders of Israel. We realize that there are within and outside Israel courageous and honorable Jewish people who do not condone the Israeli government's policy of repression, massacres, expansion, settlement and expulsion and who recognize the equal rights of our people to life, freedom, and independence. On behalf of the Palestinian people, I thank them for their courageous and honorable stance.

Our people does not want a right which is not its own or which has [not been] vested in it by international legitimacy and international law. It does not seek its freedom at the expense of anyone else's freedom, nor does it want a destiny which negates the destiny of another people. Our people refuses to be better or worse than any other people. Our people wants to be the equal of all other peoples, with the same rights and obligations. I call upon all peoples of the world, especially those which were afflicted by the Nazi occupation and considered it their duty to close the chapter of coercion and oppression by one people against another and to lend a willing hand to all the victims of terrorism, fascism, and Nazism, to see clearly today the responsibilities cast upon them by history toward our downtrodden people which wants its children to have a place under the sun in their homeland—a place where they can live in freedom, like the rest of the children of the world.

The Palestinian Dilemma

Mr. President:

It is cause for optimism that our struggle should culminate in the ongoing *intifadah* when the international atmosphere is marked by a serious and sustained quest for international detente, accord, and progress. We are heartened by the successes scored by the United Nations and its secretary-general in contributing effectively to settling many problems and defusing trouble spots around the world in this new environment of international detente.

Surely, it is impossible to consolidate this new, positive international climate without addressing problems and trouble spots around the globe. This would enable us to formulate a more accurate and reliable yardstick to assess the endeavors of man and nations and to brace for the next century and the challenges and new responsibilities it will lay before us in terms of averting wars and destruction and promoting more freedom, well-being, peace, and progress for mankind.

No one, Mr. President, would dispute the fact that the Palestine problem is the problem of our contemporary world. It is the oldest on your agenda. It is the most intricate and complex. Of the regional issues, it poses the most serious threat to international peace and security. Hence, its priority among the issues that should command the attention of the two superpowers and all the countries of the world. Hence, the need for an effort to outline a course for its equitable solution—a solution that would spread peace across the Middle East. . . .

It pleases me to inform you, with great pride, that our Palestine National Council, through a totally free exercise of democracy, has again demonstrated its ability to shoulder its national responsibilities, endorsing serious constructive and responsible resolutions which pave the way for us to reinforce and highlight our desire and contribution to find a peaceful settlement that would secure the national and political rights of our people as well as peace and security for everyone else.

Defining the Palestinian State

Mr President:

The first and decisive resolution of our Palestine National Council was the proclamation of the establishment of the State of Palestine, with the holy city of Jerusalem [al-Quds ash-Sharif) as its Capital. The State of Palestine was declared:

- By virtue of the Palestinian Arab people's natural historic, and legal right to their homeland, Palestine, and of the sacrifices of their successive generations in defense of the liberty and independence of their homeland;
- Pursuant to the resolutions of the Arab summit conference,
- By the authority of international legitimacy, as embodied in the resolutions of the United Nations since 1947;
- In implementation of the Palestinian Arab people's right to self-determination, political independence, and sovereignty on their soil, and in conformity with your Successive resolutions.

It is important for me, in repeating this historic proclamation before the international community, now that it has become one of the official United Nations documents to reaffirm that this decision is irreversible and that we will not relent until it succeeds in casting off the occupation, enabling our Palestinian people wherever they may be to exercise their sovereignty in their state, the State of Palestine. In it they shall develop their national and cultural identity and enjoy full equality in rights. Their religious and political beliefs and their human dignity shall be safeguarded under a democratic parliamentary system of government built on freedom of opinion; the freedom to form parties; the protection of the rights of the minority by the majority and respect for the decision of the majority by the minority; social justice and equal rights, free of ethnic, religious, racial, or sexual discrimination; a constitution that guarantees the rule of law and the independence of the judiciary; and on the basis of total allegiance to the centuries-old spiritual and civilizational Palestinian heritage of religious tolerance and coexistence.

The State of Palestine is an Arab State; its people are an integral part of the Arab nation and of the nation's heritage, its civilization, and its aspiration to attain its goals of social progress, unity and liberation. [The State of Palestine] is committed to the Charter of the League of Arab States, the United Nations Charter, the Universal Declaration of Human Rights, and the principles of non-alignment.

It is a peace-loving state committed to the principles of peaceful coexistence and it shall strive with all states and peoples to attain a permanent peace built on justice and respect of rights.

It is a state which believes in the settlement of international and regional disputes by peaceful means in accordance with the charter and resolutions of the United Nations. It rejects threats of force, violence, terrorism, or the use of these against its territorial integrity and political independence, or against the territorial integrity of any other state, without prejudice to its natural right to defend its territory and independence.

It is a state which believes that the future can only bring security to those who are just or have come back to justice. This, Mr. President, is the State of Palestine which we proclaimed and which we shall endeavor to embody so that it can take its place among the states of the world and share creatively in shaping a free world where justice and peace prevail. Our state, God willing, shall have its provisional government at the earliest possible opportunity. The PNC has mandated the PLO Executive Committee to assume the functions of the said government in the interim.

PNC Demands

To embody the aforementioned decision, our Palestine National Council adopted a series of resolutions. I am keen to spotlight the most salient of these, which underline our serious determination to pursue the path of an equitable peaceful settlement and to exert maximum effort to ensure its success.

Our PNC reaffirmed the necessity of convening an international conference on the issue of the Middle East and its core, the Palestinian issue, under the auspices of the United Nations and with the participation of the permanent members of the Security Council and all parties to the conflict in the region, including, on an equal footing, the Palestine Liberation

Organization, the sole, legitimate representative of the Palestinian people, on the understanding that the international conference will be held on the basis of Security Council resolutions 242 and 338 and the safeguarding of the legitimate national and political rights of the Palestinian people, foremost among which is its right to self-determination.

Our PNC reasserted the need for Israel's withdrawal from all the Palestinian and Arab territories it occupied in 1967, including Arab Jerusalem; the establishment of the Palestinian state; the annulment of all expropriation and annexation measures; and the dismantling of the settlements established by Israel in the Palestinian and Arab territories since 1967, as called for in the Arab summit resolutions of Fez and Algiers.

Our PNC also reaffirmed the necessity [of] seeking to place the occupied Palestinian territories, including Arab Jerusalem, under the supervision of the United Nations for a limited Period, to protect our people to create an atmosphere conducive to the success of the proceedings of the international conference toward the attainment of a comprehensive political settlement and the achieve-ment of peace and security for all peoples and states in the Middle East, on the basis of mutual consent, and to enable the State of Palestine to exercise its effective authority in these territories reaffirmed earlier by the resolutions of the Arab summits.

Our PNC called for the settlement of the issue of Palestinian refuge, in accordance with the pertinent United Nations resolutions, it guaranteed freedom of worship and the right to engage in religion rites for all faiths in the holy places in Palestine. And it reconfirmed that the relationship between the fraternal Jordanian and Palestinian peoples is a privileged one and that the future relationship between the State of Palestine and the Hashemite Kingdom of Jordan will be built on confederal foundations, on the basis of the two fraternal people's free and voluntary choice, in consolidation of the historic ties that bind them and the vital interests they hold in common. The PNC reaffirmed the need for the Security Council to draw up and guarantee arrangements for security and peace between all the states that are parties to the conflict in the region.

It is important for me, Mr. President, to point out that these resolutions, in their content and wording, reflect our firm desire for peace and freedom, and our total awareness of the climate of international detente and of the eagerness of international community to achieve balanced solutions that address the claims and fundamental interests of the parties in conflict. These resolutions attest to the solemnity of the Palestinian people's position on the question of peace; that they are committed to peace and believe that it should be secured and guaranteed by the security council under the aegis of the United Nations. These resolutions constitute a firm, unambiguous response to all arguments, prejudices, stands, and pretexts used by some nations to cast doubt on the position and policy of the Palestine Liberation Organization . . .

There Can Be No More Waiting

Mr. President:

Our Palestine National Council has reaffirmed its commitment to the UN resolutions that uphold the right of peoples to resist foreign occupation, colonialism, and racial discrimination, and their right to struggle for independence. It has also reaffirmed its rejection of terrorism, in all its forms, including state terrorism, emphasizing its commitment to its past resolutions in this regard, to the resolution of the Arab summit in Algiers in 1988, to UN resolutions 421159 of 1987 and 61/40 of 1985, and to what was stated on this subject in the Cairo Declaration of 7 November 1985.

The position, Mr. President, is clear and free of all ambiguity. And yet, I, as chairman of the Palestine Liberation Organization, hereby once more declare that I condemn terrorism in all its forms, and at the same time salute those sitting before me in this hall who, in the days when they fought to free their countries from the yoke of colonialism, were accused of terrorism by their oppressors, and who today are the faithful leaders of their peoples, stalwart champions of justice and freedom. . . .

Mr. President, Honorable Members:

The situation in our Palestinian homeland can bear no more waiting. Our people and our children, leading our march to liberty, holding aloft the torch of freedom, are being martyred daily for the sake of ending the occupation and laying the foundation of peace in their free, independent homeland and in the region as a whole.

For this reason, the Palestine National Council, taking into consideration the circumstances of the Palestinians and the Israelis and the need for a spirit of tolerance between them, built its resolutions on foundations of realism.

The United Nations bears an historic, extraordinary responsibility toward our people and their rights. More than forty years ago, the United Nations, in its Resolution 181, decided on the establishment of two states in Palestine, one Palestinian Arab and the other Jewish. Despite the historic wrong that was done to our people, it is our view today that the said resolution continues to meet the requirements of international legitimacy which guarantee the Palestinian Arab people's right to sovereignty and national independence.

The acceleration of the peace process in the region requires special efforts on the part of the international community, particularly the United States and the Soviet Union, who bear a great responsibility toward the cause of peace in our region.

The Palestinian Peace Initiative

The United Nations, the permanent members of the Security Council, and all international blocs and bodies have a vital role to play at this stage. In my capacity as chairman of the PLO Executive Committee, presently assuming the functions of the provisional government of the State of Palestine, I therefore present the following Palestinian peace initiative:

First: That a serious effort be made to convene, under the supervision of the secretary-general of the United Nations, the preparatory committee of the international conference for peace in the Middle East—in accordance with the initiative of President Gorbachev and president Mitterand, which President Mitterand presented to your assembly toward the end of last September and which was supported by many states—to pave the way for the convening of the international conference, which commands universal support except from the government of Israel.

Second: In view of our belief in international legitimacy and the vital role of the United Nations, that actions be undertaken to place our occupied Palestinian land under temporary United Nations supervision, and that international forces be deployed there to protect our people and, at the same time, to supervise the withdrawal of the Israeli forces from our country.

Third: The PLO will seek a comprehensive settlement among the parties concerned in the Arab-Israeli conflict, including the State of Palestine, Israel, and other neighbors, within the framework of the international conference for peace in the Middle East on the basis of resolutions 242 and 338 and so as to guarantee equality and the balance of interests, especially our people's rights, in freedom, national independence, and respect the right to exist in peace and security for all.

If these principles are endorsed at the international conference, we will have come a long way toward a just settlement, and this will enable us to reach agreement on all security and peace arrangements.

Mr. President:

I hope it is clear to everyone that our Palestinian people, determined though they are to gain their legitimate national rights to self-determination, repatriation, and the ending of the occupation of the Palestinian state's territory, are equally determined to strive for those goals by peaceful means within the framework of the international conference under the sponsorship of the United Nations and in accordance with its charter and resolutions. . . .

So let the voices supporting the olive branch, peaceful co-existence, and international entente be heard. Let all hands join in defense of an historic, possibly irreplaceable opportunity to put an end to a tragedy that has lingered too long and cost thousands of lives and the destruction of hundreds of village and cities. We reach for the olive branch because it sprouts in our hearts from the tree of the homeland, the tree of freedom.

Mr. President, Honorable Members:

I come to you in the name of my people, offering my hands that we can make true peace, peace based on justice. I ask the leaders of Israel to come here, under the sponsorship of the United Nations, so that together, we can forge that peace. I say to them, as I say to you, that our people, who want dignity, freedom, and peace for themselves and security for their state, want the same things for all the states and parties involved in the Arab-Israeli conflict. And here, I would address myself specifically to the Israeli people in all their parties and forces, and especially to the advocates of democracy and peace among them. I say to them: Come, let us make peace. Cast away fear and intimidation. Leave behind the specter of the wars that have raged continuously in the furnace of this conflict for the past forty years. Set aside all threats of wars to come, whose fuel could only be the bodies of our children and yours. Come, let us make peace.

Enough of Blood and Tears

Yitzhak Rabin

For many people in the early 1990s, Israeli prime minister Yitzhak Rabin was considered the greatest hope for peace the region had ever seen. Rabin had turned from his hawkish past in the Israeli Defense Forces (IDF) to work passionately with the Palestinians in ending the bloodshed of the intifida and creating a lasting peace. The intifida began in 1987 when Rabin was defense minister for Israel. It involved major riots and civilian-led revolts in Palestinian towns in the West Bank and Gaza in response to Israeli occupation that had gone unchecked since the 1967 war. It cost many Palestinian lives and badly hurt Israel's image in the international arena.

While much of the world was distracted by the Gulf War in 1991, Israel and the Palestine Liberation Organization (PLO) met secretly in Oslo, Norway. The conference led to the signing of the Declaration of Principles at the White House in September 1993. Within this declaration, Israel recognized the PLO as the representative for the Palestinians and the PLO recognized Israel's right to exist, accepted UN resolutions 242 and 338, and promised to abandon the use of violence and terrorism. Rabin gave the following speech upon the signing of the agreement. The Declaration of Principles led to further negotiations with the PLO, specifically in trying to define Palestinian autonomy as well as improving relations with Jordan and the United States. In 1994, Rabin was awarded the Nobel Peace Prize along with Shimon Peres and Yasser Arafat for their efforts. It seemed like lasting

Yitzhak Rabin, statement at the signing of the Declaration of Principles, Washington, D.C., September 13, 1993.

peace would finally be achieved, but in November 1995, Rabin was assassinated by a militant Israeli critical of conciliatory relations with the PLO. Peace had yet to take hold.

This signing of the Israeli-Palestinian Declaration of Principles here today is not so easy, neither for myself as a soldier in Israel's wars, nor for the people of Israel nor for the Jewish people in the Diaspora [outside of Israel] who are watching us now with great hope mixed with apprehension. It is certainly not easy for the families of the victims of the wars, violence, terror, whose pain will never heal, for the many thousands who defended our lives with their own and have even sacrificed their lives for our own. For them, this ceremony has come too late.

Today, on the eve of an opportunity for peace, and perhaps an end to violence and wars, we remember each and every one of them with everlasting love. We have come from Jerusalem, the ancient and eternal capital of the Jewish People. We have come from an anguished and grieving land. We have come from a people, a home, a family that has not known a single year, not a single month, in which mothers have not wept for their sons. We have come to try and put an end to the hostilities so that our children, and our children's children, will no longer experience the painful cost of war, violence and terror. We have come to secure their lives and to ease the sorrow and the painful memories of the past, to hope and pray for peace.

Let me say to you, the Palestinians, we are destined to live together on the same soil in the same land. We, the soldiers who have returned from battles stained with blood; we who have seen our relatives and friends killed before our eyes; we who have attended their funerals and cannot look into the eyes of their parents; we who have come from a land where parents bury their children; we who have fought against you, the Palestinians, we say to you in a loud and clear voice, "Enough of blood and tears. Enough!"

We have no desire for revenge. We harbor no hatred towards you. We, like you, are people—people who want to build a home, to plant a tree, to love, live side by side with you in dignity, in affinity, as human beings, as free men. We are today giving peace a chance and saying again to you, "Enough." Let us pray that a day will come when we will all say farewell to arms. We wish to open a new chapter in the sad book of our lives together—a chapter of mutual recognition, of good neighborliness, of understanding. We hope to embark on a new era in the history of the Middle East.

Today here in Washington at the White House, we will begin a new reckoning in the relations between peoples, between parents tired of war, between children who will not know war. Mr. President of the United States, ladies and gentlemen, our inner strength, our higher moral values have been derived for thousands of years from the Book of Books, in one of which, *Koheleth* (Ecclesiastes), we read, "To every thing there is a season, and a time to every purpose under heaven. A time to be born and a time to die, . . . a time to kill and a time to heal. . . . A time to weep and a time to laugh. A time to love, and a time to hate, a time of war and a time of peace." Ladies and gentlemen, the time of peace has come.

GREAT
SPEECHES
IN
HISTORY

An
Uncertain
Peace

Israel Has Chosen War over Peace

Yasser Arafat

Starting with the Sharm el-Sheikh Memorandum in 1999, Yasser Arafat and Israeli prime minister Ehud Barak attempted to revive the Oslo agreements after they stalled in the mid-1990s. In 2000 U.S. president Bill Clinton invited Arafat and Barak to Camp David (dubbed Camp David II) to forge a final settlement. For the first time, Israel was willing to offer part of East Jerusalem as a Palestinian capital, but talks ended over the question of Palestinian refugees. In January 2001 negotiators met again at Taba in Egypt to iron out the agreements of Camp David II. Barak's popularity was sliding and he was facing a difficult election in February. But the Taba talks seemed to be going well. On January 28 Israeli foreign minister Ben Ami stated publicly that "peace in our time" was just weeks away. Twenty-four hours later, Arafat gave this speech at the World Economic Forum in Davos, Switzerland.

Arafat decided to speak strongly about politics, noting how the Palestinian economy had been destroyed by the Israeli occupation. In the speech, Arafat points out how Israel has denied Palestine the building of vital economic infrastructures. While many held Arafat responsible for inciting the second intifada, or popular revolt in Palestine, Arafat asserts in this speech that it is Israel that has been waging a "savage and barbaric war" against the Palestinians, even accusing them of using ammunitions containing depleted uranium. He continues his address to the international community, detailing the suffering of Palestinian children, hoping the world will put pressure on Israel to

Yasser Arafat, address to the World Economic Forum, Davos, Switzerland, January 28, 2001.

protect and promote the Palestinian cause.

Israeli minister Shimon Peres shared the stage with Arafat at Davos. He had just delivered a speech promoting peace in the region and felt deeply insulted. He decided not to respond to Arafat's acerbic speech. The next day Ehud Barak announced he was suspending all negotiations with Arafat until after elections in Israel. In the elections, Barak's hardliner opponent, Ariel Sharon, won by a landslide.

Allow me first, Mr. President, to convey to you, a special greeting on convening this important economic forum. I would like to express to you, as well, our sincerest thanks and our deepest appreciation for your kind invitation to this gathering in this year. I highly appreciate the efforts you have undertaken in the planning for and the organization of bringing together this important number of experienced personalities and decision makers the world over.

For years, we have participated in your Forum. We are doing it today, because we believe that the Davos Forum is important and because it contributes to comprehensive economic and social development on the regional and international levels. It is a forum where the horizons of positive and constructive cooperation as well as the interaction among the economies of the various countries take place. This happens through developing economic and trade relations based on participation, exchange of experiences and mutual benefit to the best of the common interests of the countries and institutions participating in this Forum. This is done in a way that creates a positive economic atmosphere among states, delegations and institutions. This in turn, fosters the already existing economic and trade relations and founds for new horizons of economic and trade cooperation and exchange, and contributes, in a valuable manner, to the development and growth of the world economy as a whole. It leaves good repercussions on the levels of income for individuals and societies.

When we talk about economics, there is no way but to talk about politics because of its great influence on economics. The relationship between the two is a dialectical one. The influence of the political situation on the life and economy of any nation, people or country is a huge one—indeed it is quintessential and decisive.

You know, ladies and gentlemen, how many tiring efforts we have undertaken, to raise our Palestinian economy that was handed over to us totally destroyed by the Israeli occupation. There were no institutions and no infrastructures. The whole economy of the Occupied Palestinian Territory poured into the Israeli treasury. There was no existence of any projects or institutions for the development of the Palestinian economy and society. Israel was set on exploiting all of our economic and natural resources in the interest of the economy of its occupation. This left negative repercussions and destructive consequences on our economy.

Over seven years of hard and continuous labor, we worked to create an economic environment conducive to investment, development and growth. We made big efforts to establish our institutions and the necessary infrastructures. From here, I would like to thank all our brothers and friends, for the help they have extended to the Palestinian people. It is a help that assisted us in making the projects of economic development and growth succeed, despite what we faced in terms of obstacles, impediments and difficulties, which Israel had, and still does, put in the face of our developing economy.

Israel has delayed the operational functioning of the airport. It has not allowed us to start building the seaport. As you know, these two, the airport and the seaport, are important and vital institutions. In addition, Israel has obstructed other projects, important to our economy and to our people e.g. the electricity and water and other projects. The Government of Barak, as well as the preceding Government of [Benjamin] Netanyahu, practiced the policy of economic strangulations, closures and siege, as well as starvation and collective punishment against our Palestinian people.

The current Government of Israel is waging, for the last four months, a savage and barbaric war, as well as a blatant and fascist military aggression against our Palestinian people. In this aggression it is using internationally prohibited weapons and ammunitions that include in their construction

depleted uranium. In addition, Israel is laying against us total siege, indeed, worse than that, it is imposing this siege
against every village and town. It is prohibiting the freedom
of movement and travel of our people. It is jeopardizing the
basic human rights of our Palestinian citizens, dismissing our
workers, closing our factories, destroying a number of these,
so much so that 90% of our workers are forcibly unem-
ployed, destroying our farms and fruit trees and prohibiting
export and import, indeed it is forbidding us to receive, from
brothers and friends, donated provisions. All this is in violation of all resolutions of international legality, the Universal
Declaration of Human Rights, International Human Law
and the Fourth Geneva Convention relating to the Protection
of Civilians in Times of War.

Have you seen a more ugly policy than this policy of collective punishment or more destruction in the contemporary
age? Israel is putting all of our people in confrontation with
this dangerous military escalation, and its occupational, settlement, aggressive and armed expansionism as well as in
confrontation with its dreams of achieving territorial and regional gains at the expense of our people, in a manner, which
is in contravention of international legality and the rights of
our Palestinian people to their land, Christian and Islamic
holy places and to their natural resources.

Mr. President,

Ladies and Gentlemen, leaders and members of the delegations,

Whoever wants really to achieve peace and seeks it with
belief and sincerity, does not resort to killing, persecution, assassination, destruction and devastation as the Government
of Israel and its army of occupation are doing to our people
these days and since four continuous months. The number of
Palestinian martyrs has exceeded . . . four hundred. The number of injured persons has exceeded seventeen thousand, of
whom 5439 are children. These are the human losses and
damages. The grand total, so far, of the economic and financial losses in all sectors, as a result of destruction caused by
the Israeli occupational military machine, to the infrastructures and to public and private property and other losses is US
$2.4 billion including the heavy losses inflicted on the Pales-

tinian farmers as a result of cutting more than one hundred thousand trees and leveling of 10000 dunums of land (1 dunum = 1000 square meters). This, of course, leaves destructive consequences on the livelihood of the Palestinian citizens and the Palestinian investment. Added to these losses should be those caused by the Israeli shells, from tanks, artillery, planes and rockets, to the buildings, establishments, installations and institutions, such as schools, colleges, churches and mosques.

This is a very short resume of what has befallen our society in terms of dire human and material losses and as a result of the situation of total siege and closure. As a result, the percentage of those who are living under the line of poverty has risen to 75% and general national income has decreased sharply in millions of US dollars annually.

Palestine Is Dedicated to Peace and Justice

While we confirm to you, dear friends once more, our adherence to a comprehensive, just and permanent peace, the peace of the brave, as a firm strategic choice of our Palestinian people, we look up to you, and to the United Nations and to all justice-, freedom-, peace- and democracy-loving forces the world over, and to all brothers and friends, to approach the vital and influential international forces in the world, so as to bear their moral and human responsibilities in order to work in sincerity, objectivity, neutrality and fairness, to find a quick and just solution to the Issue of Palestine, in accordance with the spirit of right and justice and the international resolutions related to Palestine.

You know, ladies and gentlemen, that we have made great concessions and sacrifices in order to achieve comprehensive, just and permanent peace. Yes, indeed, we have accepted less than one quarter of the total area of historic Palestine. We accepted, at the Madrid Peace Conference, the principle of land for peace on the basis of [UN] Security Council Resolutions 242 and 338 which call for the withdrawal of Israel, the occupying power, from all Arab and Palestinian occupied territories, including Holy Jerusalem, to the fourth of June border lines; the dismantling of every thing the occupation has built in terms of settlements and settlement structures that have no basis of legality; and the implementation of [UN General Assembly] Resolution 194 on the Palestinian refugees. We have achieved, as well, peace agreements with my late partner Yitzhak Rabin, in making the peace of the brave, which guarantees us the establishment of our independent Palestinian state, with holy Jerusalem as its capital.

We look forward to the whole international community, the United Nations Organization and the vital and influential international forces, to work for ending this Israeli war and aggression against our unarmed people; a war and an aggression which constitute a flagrant and blatant violation of the Fourth Geneva Convention relating to the Protection of Civilians in Times of War. We ask for the provision of international protection for our people immediately, the lifting of the siege and closure and the ending of this escalating military aggression.

Our Palestinian people, ladies and gentlemen, look up to you to help them in realizing their inalienable legitimate national rights so as to be able to march forward on the road of development and construction of their homeland, to catch up with the developed and advanced course of international economy, and to live with dignity, freedom, sovereignty and independence in their homeland, Palestine, like all other peoples and states in the region and the world, in a framework of confidence, mutual respect and good neighborliness with their surroundings.

Finally, we reiterate our thanks to you, Mr. President, for inviting us, and for giving us the opportunity to address this august Forum. We wish you success and good luck in realizing the noble aims of this meeting. We express our sincere hope and firm desire to have the honor to invite you all on a very close day, God be willing, to convene your Forum in Holy Jerusalem, the capital of the independent State of Palestine.

Peace be with you all.

The Palestinian Response to Camp David II

Abu Mazen

In late 2000 representatives of Israel and the Palestinian Authority (PA) met at Camp David, Maryland, with U.S. president Bill Clinton acting as mediator. Many believe this is the closest the two parties have ever come to hammering out a comprehensive peace agreement. At the meeting, which was named Camp David II, both sides seemed willing to make key concessions that had previously never even reached the bargaining table. Many consider Yasser Arafat's speech at Davos the reason for this summit's failure—signaling a Palestinian withdrawal from the negotiations right before the Israeli election. This election saw Ariel Sharon come into power. Sharon demanded an end to all Palestinian terrorist actions before the resumption of talks.

This speech of September 9, 2001, by the Palestine Liberation Organization's (PLO) chief negotiator Abu Mazen (or Mahmoud Abbas), speaks against the assumption that it was the PLO who pulled out of the Camp David II agreements. The members of the PLO maintain they agreed to the general outline of the summit but needed more time to hammer out the details, at least until April 2000. The date was unacceptable to Sharon and Israel.

Mazen recounts the Palestinian perspective on these crucial talks, specifically the differences in opinion between Israel and the Palestinians regarding security, borders, Jerusalem, and—possibly the most contentious—the

Abu Mazen, address at the meeting of the Palestinian Central Council, September 9, 2001.

issue of evicted refugees. He is speaking to the PLO's
Central Council, informing them of the Palestinian's position and how he and the other negotiators plan to move
forward in the process. After serving many years in the
PLO under Arafat, working as chief negotiator lent him
international recognition. This led Abbas to be the natural selection for the new position of Palestinian prime
minister in 2003, a power-sharing agreement with Arafat
that was highly encouraged by Western powers.

We went to Camp David carrying our well-known
positions, positions that were adopted by several
of our legislative bodies. The positions we adopted
are, in our point of view, the minimum that we can accept.
They are positions that are based on United Nations Resolutions 242, 338 and 194. They are based on agreements
signed between the Israelis and us, they are based on Israeli
documents concerning the 1948 nakba (catastrophe) and the
forced expulsion of Palestinians from their homes, and they
are based on UN Security Council resolutions dealing with
Jerusalem and Jewish settlements.

We stressed to the Americans that for a summit at such a
level to succeed it must be prepared for and prepared for
well. We cautioned that because of the lack of preparation
the prospect of its failure is high. The Americans agreed that
a summit at this level needed preparation and they agreed
with us that time must be given for preparations. We agreed
with Secretary [Madeleine] Albright that we would have two
weeks to prepare. We were later surprised by a telephone call
from President Clinton inviting us to a summit that was to be
held within a week.

Why We Went to Camp David

We were faced with two choices, to go knowing very well
that the summit will fail and that the Americans may blame
us for its failure, or to refuse to attend and be accused of sab-
otaging the peace process. So we took the first choice.

We went to Camp David not to say NO to the Americans and the world Zionists. We went to say YES to a lasting and just peace. To say YES to international legitimacy and when we failed to reach that, we said NO. Again, we did not go to Camp David to not reach an agreement or to reject points for the sake of rejection so that it would be said that we stood strong. We went to reach an agreement; we dealt with every issue with a strong desire to reach an agreement that would end this conflict that has lasted the entire century.

To assist us in this effort we brought to Camp David eight young, bright legal advisors and maps experts who, on request were ready to present documentation and advise which they had been preparing for such occasions. We feel very proud of these fine, energetic lawyers in who we have great trust and are very happy to have on our side.

Through the Americans the Israelis presented their vision on Jerusalem. They envisioned a Jerusalem where some villages around the city would come under Palestinian sovereignty. Neighborhoods outside the walls of the Old City would remain under Israeli sovereignty with the Palestinians having some type of self-rule. The quarters inside the Old City would be divided. The Jewish and Armenian Quarters will be sliced away from the Muslim and Christian Quarters, which will be ruled under a special system. In their attempt to sell this to the Palestinians, they threw in sovereign headquarters for the Palestine President inside the Old City.

Israel refused to accept moral and legal responsibility for the plight of the refugees. Israel only showed willingness to allow several hundreds to return every year on humanitarian causes. As for compensation, Israel said any fund that will be established would also compensate Jews who left Arab countries.

On borders, Israel demanded control over the Palestinian borders with Jordan and Egypt. Israel also asked to control 15–20 percent of the Jordan River and a sector of the Jordan Valley. Israel also wants to annex 10.5 percent of the West Bank to absorb the settlements. But all West Bank settlements do not sit on more than 1.8 percent.

Israel says it needs 3–5 army bases for monitoring and intervention purposes. Israel also demands that the air space be completely under its control. It asked for a presence at all international entry points to monitor persons, products and weapons. As for the state of Palestine, it must be a demilitarized state.

Summary of the Issues

If we were to summarize the positions of both the Palestinians and Israelis it would be as follows:

Security:

The Israelis want control over a part of the Jordan Valley for a maximum 12-year period. That would keep the current military bases and settlements there untouched. The Israelis asked for six bases in the West Bank and three military monitoring areas. Israel demanded it have a presence at the international crossings (to monitor those entering and leaving the area). Israel also demanded the entire air space and electromagnetic space to be under its control. The Palestinians said they would accept an international force or a multi-national force on the borders. What we won't accept is an Israeli presence, in any form on Palestinian territory.

Borders:

Israel wants to carve out 15–20 percent of the Jordan River and Dead Sea border and to annex 10.5 percent of West Bank Land. The Palestinians rejected any carving of borders. Light border amendments and an exchange of lands equal in quantity and quality that does not exceed 2 percent is acceptable.

Refugees:

The Israelis agree to contribute to an international fund to be established for the compensation of Palestinian refugees. However, Israel wants the fund to compensate Jews who came to the country from Arab states. Israel agrees to the return of hundreds of refugees under a family reunification plan or on humanitarian cases. The Palestinians want Israel to take moral and legal responsibility for the refugee crisis. UN Resolution 194 must be accepted so that all refugees are guaranteed the right of return, and by return we mean to Israel. Refugees who choose to return and those who do not must be compensated. The Absentee Treasurer created in Israel in 1949 to administer refugee money is responsible for the compensation. Host countries should also be compensated. An international fund could be established but that fund would only be responsible for part of the compensation. We refuse to mix the issue of Palestinian refugees with Jewish immigrants.

Jerusalem:

Jerusalem, occupied in 1967, is the city within the walls that includes the Haram al-Sharif, the Holy Sepulcher, and the Muslim, Christian, and Armenian quarters. It is also the city outside the walls, with neighborhoods like Sheikh Jarrah. Musrara, Damascus Gate, Saleh Eldin Street and others. The Israeli position divides Jerusalem into several sections and gave each section a different legal status.

1) The walled city: The Haram al-Sharif: Israel to have sovereignty and the Palestinians will be given guardianship of the Muslim, Christian, and Armenian Quarters: to remain under Israeli sovereignty A Palestinian presidential complex inside the Muslim Quarter that will be given sovereign power.

2) Outside the walled city: sovereignty remains with Israel with municipal functions over these neighborhoods to be carried out by the municipality of Abu Dis. With the exception of two villages, villages surrounding Jerusalem, most of which are area B, will come under Palestinian sovereignty. Israel will have a road that runs through the villages linking them to areas under their sovereignty. The Palestinians will only have one road linking them to the Haram.

The Palestinian Position

All of east Jerusalem should be returned to Palestinian sovereignty. The Jewish Quarter and Western Wall should be placed under Israeli authority not Israeli sovereignty. An open city and cooperation on municipal services.

This is our summary of the results of the Camp David negotiations. But the Israelis had a different understanding that was revealed in subsequent local meetings. Israel wants 10.5 percent of the West Bank and rejects the idea of a land exchange. Israel wants 5 monitoring posts with three roads leading to them. Three Israeli administered early warning systems with a Palestinian liaison officer present at the stations. Israeli control over 8 percent of the Jordan Valley for a 12–15 year period. No right of return to Israel. Israel may accept the return of 10,000 Palestinians over a 15-year period under a family reunification plan. Air space to come under Palestinian sovereignty but will be controlled by Israel through guiding systems. An end to the conflict A demilitarized Palestinian state Jerusalem: The same position as in Camp David.

This is the Israeli position as told to us ten days ago. It shows that there are fundamental differences in the positions and that the gaps between the two sides remain very wide.

A declaration of an independent state is a right our people can execute at any time. In 1988, when we declared our state in exile, more than 100 countries recognized that declaration. But recognition of a state on the ground is different that that of a state in exile. And though many nations have said they are in favor of an independent state many hinted of the necessity to declare once prepared on the ground and or after an agreement between the sides is reached. And so we must now stop and think.

Committing to a date has its positive side, it shows that dates and promise are respected and kept, but such a commitment must be based on good preparations not emotional reactions.

We need to carefully study the Israeli response to the declaration. If Israel were to respond negatively, we need to study what measures she will take and how will we respond to these measures.

A Gradual, Controlled Peace

Ariel Sharon

Every year the Israeli Institute of Policy and Strategy (IPS) hosts the Herzliya Conference on the campus of the Herzliya Interdisciplinary Center in Herzliya, Israel. Prime Minister Ariel Sharon gave this speech at the third annual conference. Sharon was voted into office in February 2001. His tenure as prime minister saw the deaths of thousands of Israelis and Palestinians as the second intifada raged with terrorist attacks against Israelis and Sharon's hard-line government responded with overwhelming force. In this speech, Sharon insists he is dedicated to the peace process. However, he admits that his methodology is different from past Israeli prime ministers. He backs a limited, gradual process, making sure small agreements are accepted and implemented before moving forward. Considered a hawkish, pro-war, politician, Sharon is making an appeal to both his conservative party and the more liberal parties in Israel with this address.

Sharon admits his decision to begin talks with the Palestinians comes after intense pressure from the United States which saw progress in the Arab-Israeli conflict necessary to ensure support for military action in Iraq. However, like the administration of George W. Bush, Sharon's willingness to work with the Palestinian Authority (PA) is contingent upon new Palestinian leadership. He believes that Arafat has outlived his usefulness to the peace process. While Arafat, unsurprisingly, scoffed at this, it became clear to many in the world that the PA might need a new face if progress would ever be made toward

Ariel Sharon, address before the Herzliya Conference, Herzliya, Israel, December 4, 2002.

peace. Perhaps fearing neglect, Arafat soon appointed Mahmoud Abbas, a long-time friend and ally, as Palestinian prime minister to work out the details for peace accords with Israel and the West. Seizing on the change in leadership, Ariel Sharon surprised the world in May 2003 by announcing that Israel must end its occupation of Palestinian territories.

Twenty-seven months ago the Palestinian Authority commenced a campaign of terror against the State of Israel. Since then, we have been confronting a ferocious battle against a culture of bloodshed and murder, which has targeted Jews and Israelis everywhere. This campaign of terror was not coincidental; it was meticulously planned and prepared by the Chairman of the Palestinian Authority who misconstrued the high regard for human life in Israeli society as a way to compel us to capitulate to terrorism and coerce us into additional political concessions, concession with nothing in return.

The past two years have been a difficult and painful test for Israel's national strength. The callousness and brutality of the terrorists was aimed—first and foremost—at undermining the sense of justness of the people of Zion. This is not the place to ask what led the PA Chairman to question the inner strength and determination which has always characterized the citizens of Israel, but it is clear that the terror has not defeated and will never defeat the State of Israel. They tried to break our spirit—and failed. This failure has resulted in scathing Palestinian criticism of Arafat, his path of terrorism and ongoing strategy of violence against Israel.

Israel and the United States

Today, most of the weight of the global leadership is in the United States. From the first days of the establishment of the State of Israel, our bond with the United States has been a supreme strategic asset. My Government has further consolidated our relations with the United States and formed a special closeness with the U.S. Administration and Congress. These special relations, the understanding of Israel's needs, and the cooperation with President Bush and his administration are unprecedented. Israel has in the United States true friends who genuinely and honestly care for our security.

Our political understandings with the United States and the Administration's understanding of our security needs have provided us with the required leeway in our ongoing war on terrorism. The war on terror has been accompanied by exorbitant costs and harsh financial damage, and I hope and believe that in the coming months we will receive special aid, to support us in our economic campaign.

On June 24th this year, President Bush presented his plan for a true solution to our conflict with the Palestinians. The peace plan outlined in the President's speech is a reasonable, pragmatic and practicable one, which offers a real opportunity to achieve an agreement. We have accepted in principle the President's plan and the sequence presented therein. Our agreements with the Palestinians are based on the lessons the Americans learned from the Clinton-Barak plan, and my experience as one who has, for many years, participated in the security and political campaign in the Palestinian arena.

The First Phase: End Terror

After concerted efforts, the U.S. Administration has understood and agreed that the only way to achieve a true peace agreement with the Palestinians is progress in phases, with the first phase being a complete cessation of terror. President Bush's speech is a fatal blow to Arafat's policy of terrorism and serves as proof of the failure of his attempt to achieve political gains by means of violence and terrorism. Only after a cessation of terror—and this is already agreed by most world leaders—will the commencement of peace negotiations between the parties be possible.

The American plan defines the parties' progress according to phases. The transition from one phase to the next will not be on the basis of a predetermined timetable—which would have resulted in a build-up of heavy pressure on Israel towards the end of one phase and approaching the next phase. Rather, progress is determined on the basis of performance—only once a specific phase has been implemented, will progress into the next phase be possible.

On the basis of lessons learned from past agreements, it is clear to all that Israel can no longer be expected to make political concessions until there is proven calm and Palestinian governmental reforms.

In this context, it is important to remember that political concessions which will be made in the future—as those made in the past—are irreversible.

Even the current security reality, with the IDF [Israel Defense Force] operating freely inside Palestinian cities, arises from security needs and has not changed the political situation of two years ago. Israel will not re-control territories from which it withdrew as a result of political agreements. Therefore, the achievement of true and genuine coexistence must be a pre-condition to any discussion on political arrangements.

The Jewish people seek peace. Israel's desire is to live in security and in true and genuine coexistence, based, first and foremost, on the recognition of our natural and historic right to exist as a Jewish state in the land of Israel, while maintaining genuine peace.

Requirements for the PA

The achievement of true coexistence must be carried out, first and foremost, by the replacement of the Palestinian leadership which has lied and disappointed, with different leadership which can—and more importantly—is willing to achieve real peace with the State of Israel. Unfortunately, there remain a few in Israel who believe that Arafat is still relevant. However, the U.S. Administration—with the world following in its footsteps—has already accepted our unequivocal position that no progress will be possible with Arafat as the Chairman of the Palestinian Authority. This man is not—and never will be—a partner to peace. He does not want peace.

The reconstruction of a Palestinian government should commence with governmental reforms which will ultimately lead to the establishment of a new, honest and peace-seeking administration, the removal of Arafat from his command of power and sources of financing, and from the decision-making process, and his relegation to a symbolic role.

In concordance with the sequence presented by President Bush, a Chief Executive Officer for Reforms will be appointed to the Palestinian Authority, and will constitute the head of the executive authority and the source of administrative authority. The provisional Palestinian government will administer a more efficient governmental system, fight the prevailing corruption in the PA and adhere to regulations of proper management. That government will lead a comprehensive process of reforms, maintain coexistence and prepare the general elections.

The elections in the Palestinian Authority should be held only at the conclusion of the reform process and after proper governmental regulations have been internalized. The goal is that these will be true elections—free, liberated and democratic.

Parallel with, and perhaps even prior to the governmental reforms, a security reform will be carried out, consisting of three principle parts:

1. Dismantling all existing security (/terrorist) bodies, the majority of which are, in fact, involved in terror; these organizations, which are directly subordinate to Arafat, are essentially corrupt, and responsible for the deaths of hundreds of Israelis. These bodies will be replaced by two or three new organizations which will consist of a police force and security services; these new organizations will have a uniform command, which will be responsible for dismantling the current complex web of militias and armed gangs.

2. A Minister of the Interior will be appointed, and will be responsible for collecting illegal weapons and transferring them to a third party which will remove them from the PA territories and destroy them, and outlawing terrorist organizations.

3. In addition, cooperation on security issues between the PA and Israel will be renewed immediately.

The security reform must accompany a sincere and real effort to stop terrorism, while applying the "chain of preventive measures" outlined by the Americans: intelligence gathering, arrest, interrogation, prosecution and punishment.

Supervising the Palestinian Economy

Another important matter is the international demand for honest, effective, non-corrupt and transparent administration of the PA financial system; it is of great importance that the PA manage its financial affairs in concordance with the rules of proper government which will obligate the Palestinian Authority, inter alia, to produce a detailed budget, under a budgetary control system. This budgetary auditing system will ensure a balance between income and expenditure, and will verify that budget spending only serves appropriate economic purposes for the benefit and welfare of the Palestinian people. Such a supervising mechanism will also prevent the transfer of money for the financing of organizations or individuals involved in terror.

Taking the financial system out of Arafat's hands, and appointing a strong Minister of Finance with authority, constitutes an important factor for stopping the terrorist system operated by the Palestinian Authority. We are hopeful that the newly appointed PA Minister of Finance will operate a body to oversee and handle foreign aid funds received by the PA, and channel those funds to clearly defined projects which will benefit the Palestinian people and which are not contaminated by terror and corruption.

Peace and coexistence cannot be achieved without reform in the fields of education, media and information; the virulent incitement mechanism instigated by the PA against Israel must be stopped immediately; there can be no peace while the Palestinian education system instills in their young generation a culture of hatred, violence and terror.

Today, there is an increasing understanding in the world that stopping the phenomenon of suicide terrorism is dependent on the cessation of incitement, ending the religious ratification of terrorism by radical elements in the Muslim world— with the encouragement and support of various Arab states.

The Palestinian justice system and law-enforcement must also undergo significant reforms. It is unheard of that in a law-abiding country, one hour after being arrested for theft, a suspect is sentenced and hanged, while on the other hand those involved in terror enter and leave prison in the "revolving door" principle. As long as those who commit crimes against the State of Israel are not severely punished, no progress will be made in President Bush's sequence.

The two sides will advance to the next phase of President Bush's sequence when a new, different, responsible and non-corrupt Palestinian leadership emerges. Terror will cease, and the Palestinian leadership will not allow it to be renewed. Civil and economic cooperation will be established. Incitement will be stopped and education towards peace will be fostered. At the same time, Israel will act to lift military pressure, create territorial continuity between Palestinian population centers, and ease daily life for the Palestinian population.

The Second Phase: Grant Statehood

The second phase of President Bush's sequence proposes the establishment of a Palestinian state with borders yet to be finalized, and which will overlap with territories A and B, except for essential security zones. This Palestinian state will be completely demilitarized. It will be allowed to maintain lightly armed police and interior forces to ensure civil order. Israel will continue to control all entries and exits to the Palestinian state, will command its airspace, and not allow it to form alliances with Israel's enemies.

As I have promised in the past, President Bush's sequence will be discussed and approved by the National Unity Government which I intend to establish after the elections, and I will do my utmost to establish as broad a National Unity Government as possible.

The Final Phase: Fix Borders

In the final phase of President Bush's sequence negotiations will be opened to determine the final status of the Palestinian state and fix its permanent borders. As I emphasized, no progress will be made from one phase to the next until such time as quiet has been restored, Palestinian rule has undergone fundamental changes, and coexistence is ensured.

We all want peace. It is not a competition over who wants peace more. We also know that entering into political negotiations for peace is the true path which will bring about acceleration of economic growth and prosperity. I have said it before, and will say it again today: Israel is prepared to make painful concessions for a true peace. However, the government under my leadership will not be seduced into believing false promises which will endanger the security of the State of Israel.

My ideological and political path is well-known to you from the many functions I was privileged to fill during my decades of public service. These decisions are not easy for me, and I cannot deny that I have doubts, reservations and fears; however, I have come to the conclusion that in the present regional and international reality Israel must act with courage to accept the political plan which I described. There are risks involved, but also enormous opportunities.

I know that there are many who will attack the political outline I have just detailed. During the last few years many of us were tempted to believe in lightning-quick solutions which would lead to the security and peace we have longed for, and that this long-lasting conflict between our two peoples could be solved by the "blade of a sword"—I am familiar with these voices from both sides of the political spectrum.

Regrettably, this is not the way things are. These methods have failed—the solution to the conflict must be gradual and controlled. We must, in all stages, act with prudence and determination, exercise judgement, and make very sure that all commitments and agreements are implemented by both sides.

It is true that this is not a shining path which will lead us to instant, magical solutions, but I am certain that only by going forward in this direction, step by step, will we be able to achieve security for the Israeli people, and reach the peace we all yearn for.

Thank you, and happy holiday.

Appendix of Biographies

H.E. Gaafar Allagany

In the 1990s H.E. Gaafar Allagany served in the United Nations as a permanent representative of the kingdom of Saudi Arabia. He is currently the Saudi government's chief spokesman in the United States, managing the Saudi embassy's information office.

Yasser Arafat

Yasser Arafat was born Mohammed Abd el-Rahman Abd el-Raouf Arafat Al-Qudwa Al-Husseini in August 1929, to a Palestinian family living in Cairo, Egypt. Through his family connections in Palestine, Arafat became a Palestinian nationalist, seeking freedom for his ancestral homeland. At the time, Palestine was a protectorate of the United Kingdom, but it was also the scene of fighting between Arabs and Jews who had settled the region. Tensions between Arabs and Jews and the British rulers escalated throughout the 1930s and 1940s. Arafat returned to Cairo, however, before the situation in Palestine reached a boiling point in 1948. During that pivotal year, the British vacated the Middle East, the Jews announced the creation of Israel, and neighboring Arab nations attacked the nascent Jewish state. Arafat tried to take part in the Arab fight by joining a volunteer militia in Egypt, but Egyptian authorities disarmed the group before they saw any action. Arafat then returned to studying engineering at a Cairo university.

By 1949 Israel had destroyed the invading Arab armies and had signed an armistice with those nations. Arafat was displeased that the Arabs would accept peace with the Jews, but he was also angered that the land that was once Palestine had been divided up between Israel, Jordan (which received control of the West Bank), and Egypt (which inherited the Gaza Strip) as a result of the conflict. Arafat joined the Egyptian army to attain military training. He left Egypt in 1957 for an engineering job in Kuwait. After two years of quiet work, he joined up with some Palestinian activists from his days in Egypt. Together they formed al-Fatah ("armed struggle"), a political organization devoted to the goal of Palestinian liberation. Through a published journal, al-Fatah argued that Palestinians could free themselves by working together without reliance upon other Arab nations. Some Palestinians—especially those who favored a unified Arab front—dismissed al-Fatah as undisciplined, reckless troublemakers. One of these critics was Ahmad Al-Shukairy, a Palestinian who, with the support of Egypt's President Gamal Abdel Nasser, founded the Palestine Liberation Organization (PLO) in 1964 to direct Palestinian freedom-fighting efforts.

In the aftermath of the 1967 Six-Day War between Israel and its old Arab enemies (Egypt, Jordan, and Syria), the Gaza Strip, the West Bank, and the Golan Heights (formerly controlled by Syria) fell into Israeli hands. Arafat and al-Fatah moved to occupied Palestine to begin guerrilla warfare against Israeli military and civilian targets. Israel retaliated and captured or killed many of al-Fatah's members. Arafat, however, eluded capture, and his stature grew in the eyes of his fellow Palestinians. In 1969 Arafat's fame allowed him to take over the reins of the PLO. The organization established its base in Jordan where it attracted many adherents. Jordan's King Hussein suspected that the PLO intended to form its own state in Jordan (since many Palestinians had fled there after the previous wars), so he used his military to force the PLO out of the nation.

In the 1970s Arafat and the PLO reorganized in Beirut, Lebanon. From there, they planned and executed effective terror campaigns against Israel. In 1974 Arafat addressed the United Nations to suggest that the august body had the power either to give Palestinians back their homeland or to ensure that the guerrilla war would continue. Three years later in a startling gesture, Egyptian president Anwar el-Sadat made the first overture for peace in the region when he began negotiating a peace with Israel. Arafat, still distrustful of Arab leaders, considered the act irrelevant to the Palestinian situation and condemned Sadat for his show of weakness. Beyond Sadat's own peace treaty, the UN could broker no other peace accords in the region, so Arafat went back to fighting.

Lebanon did not remain a safe home for the PLO, however. By the early 1980s civil conflict and an Israeli attack on Palestinian targets in Beirut forced the PLO to pull up stakes once again. Arafat fled to Tunis, leaving many faithful adherents behind. The Palestinians trapped in Lebanon suffered under massacres from Lebanese Christians and an attack from Syria. In 1987 Palestinians in the West Bank demonstrated against their Israeli occupiers during an uprising called the "first intifada." Although Arafat was now in Tunisia, the PLO network had helped organize the intifada, and its leader was linked to the uprising. Oddly, though, one year later Arafat accepted a UN resolution calling for Palestinians to renounce terrorism and recognize Israel as a sovereign nation. Arafat's move may have been unpopular with some Palestinians, but to Western eyes, it gave him the image of a statesman willing to bargain for Middle Eastern peace.

In 1991 peace talks between Israel, Arab states, and the PLO were under way. By 1993 the Israeli government under Yitzhak Rabin announced that Palestinians would have self-rule in the Gaza Strip and part of the West Bank. In 1994, Arafat immediately set up the first Palestinian government in Gaza. In December of that year, Arafat, along with Rabin and Israeli foreign minister Shimon Peres, was awarded the Nobel Peace Prize. The euphoria did not last. Palestinian dissidents felt betrayed by Arafat and called for his assassination. His partner in peace, Yitzhak Rabin, was murdered by an Israeli right-wing extremist for his part in the negotiations. The peace process slowed considerably as old hatreds reemerged and Palestinian terrorist groups conducted strikes against Israeli targets.

In 1996 Arafat was elected to lead the autonomous Palestinian Authority by a majority vote, but he began having troubles with the economy. Many Palestinians worked in Israel, but fear of terrorism prompted Israel to close its borders. Palestinian finances were in shambles. Meanwhile the peace process was still stagnant. In 2000 the PLO wanted to declare an independent state of Palestine regardless of Israel's wishes. Arafat stepped up negotiations with Israeli prime minister Ehud Barak, but even with the United States standing in as mediators, nothing was accomplished. The PLO declared that it would not yet inaugurate a Palestinian state in hopes that more talks would commence with Israel. The resulting meetings, however, were as fruitless. Conflict between Israelis and Palestinians followed, putting the negotiations on hold. With U.S. insistence, Arafat tried to quell Palestinian terrorism but to no avail. In September 2000 Ariel Sharon became Israel's new prime minister. His militant stance left little room for negotiating with Arafat, whom he considered a terrorist. In December 2001 Sharon ordered Arafat be placed under house arrest. Quickly, though, he changed his mind and ordered Arafat's compound to be leveled by military force. Though his reasons were unclear, Sharon had the Israeli army lay siege to Arafat's stronghold in Ramallah on the West Bank. Defiantly, Arafat and his loyal aides held out until the siege was lifted (due to diplomatic pressure on Israel) in April 2002. Though his compound was in ruins, Arafat emerged again as a hero to the Palestinians. Since then he has continued to cast himself as a proponent of peace while at the same time a victim of unjust Israeli aggression.

Menachem Begin

Born in Poland in 1913, Menachem Begin grew up in Brest Litovsk and attended the University of Warsaw. He was a follower of Vladimir Ze'ev Jabotinsky, the founder of the Revisionist Zionist Movement. By age nineteen, Begin was already in the leadership of the organization's youth league, Betar. During the 1930s, when Britain controlled Palestine and Jewish settlement there, Begin was an activist promoting the Zionist ideal of a Jewish state in Palestine. When the German army invaded Poland in 1939, Begin escaped eastward only to be arrested a year later by the Soviets who assumed he was a Zionist insurgent. The Soviets sentenced Begin to hard labor for eight years, but he was released after one year when it was determined that he was a Polish citizen. Begin then joined a Polish army unit that had re-formed in Russia. With his unit, he traveled to Palestine in 1942.

Begin left the Polish army in 1943 and stayed in Palestine to work in a militant underground organization bent on ridding Palestine of the British and establishing a Jewish state. When the British finally pulled out in 1948 and Israel declared its statehood, Begin founded the Herut Party (Freedom Party) and became a member of the Israeli parliament (the Knesset). Begin held his leadership role in Herut for three decades. The strongly nationalistic party opposed most concessions to Palestinians or neighboring Arab states that might jeopardize Israel. After the Six-Day War in 1967, Begin and his followers rejected the notion that Israel return the lands that the Israeli army occupied when it defeated invading Arab armies. The Knesset, run by the socialist Labor Party, eventually voted to return the occupied territories. As a result, Begin and his party quit the government in 1970. Soon after, Begin formed another party, the Likud, to oppose the majority Labor Party. His nationalistic rhetoric and political experience earned him the leadership of the Likud. In 1977 the Likud received the mandate from the Israeli people to form the next government, and Begin was made the prime minister.

While fiercely protective of Israel, Begin agreed to meet with Egyptian president Anwar el-Sadat in 1977 to discuss peace between their two countries. In September 1978 Begin and Sadat signed the Camp David Accords under the auspices of U.S. president Jimmy Carter. The historic accords and the following year's peace treaty ended three decades of fighting between Egypt and Israel. Begin and Sadat shared the Nobel Peace Prize in 1978 for their cooperation. The Likud also benefited from the peace since Begin and his party retained government control after the 1981 elections.

In 1982 Israel began its war against Lebanon. The attacks were not aimed at the Lebanese but at the Palestine Liberation Organization (PLO) that had sought asylum there. The PLO had been waging a guerrilla war in occupied Palestine and Israel since the 1970s. With the largest Arab army no longer a threat after the Camp David Accords, the Israelis focused their attention on the PLO. Not everyone in the Knesset was in favor of the war, however, and international views were critical of the government's pursuit of conflict in the region. Lacking solid support and faced with mounting casualties, Begin stepped down as prime minister in 1983. The decision came as a shock since both Begin and the Likud were still favored in Israeli opinion polls. Begin never explained his resignation, although the death of his wife Aliza the previous year and the death tolls from the war in Lebanon have been cited as influential factors. Begin spent his remaining years in seclusion. He died of complications from a heart attack in March 1992.

David Ben-Gurion

David Ben-Gurion was born David Gruen in October 1886. He grew up in Poland, which was then controlled by Czarist Russia, but he dreamed of a Jewish homeland. In 1906 he traveled to Palestine to build Jewish settlements there. With the new settlements under the threat of Arab attacks, Gruen helped organize Hashomer, a civil defense force in the Galilee region of Palestine. In 1910 he left the settlements in Galilee to join the Poalei Zion (Workers) Party in Jerusalem. Becoming more politically active, Gruen was elected chairman of the Poalei and head of its party publication. It was during this time that David Gruen adopted the Hebraic name David Ben-Gurion.

As World War I erupted, Ben-Gurion was expelled from Palestine by the Turkish army for his connections to Hashomer, which the Turks (who were allies of Germany) viewed as a possible threat. Ben-Gurion sailed to New York. There he met and married his wife, Paula. Two years later Ben-Gurion journeyed back to Palestine when Britain agreed to establish a Jewish homeland there. But the British were slow in making good on their promise. They inherited

Palestine soon after the end of World War I, but they were not eager to permit the Jews their own state due to Britain's own interests in the area and the growing anger of neighboring Arab states. Britain held on to the region until 1948, when the British government decided to vacate the area as tensions rose and the price of maintaining control became too high. It was then that the Jews in Palestine declared their independence as the new nation of Israel.

Between World War I and 1948, Ben-Gurion remained in politics and worked toward Jewish independence. He helped found the Jewish Federation of Labor in 1921 and chaired that organization for the next fourteen years. He then became head of the Labor Party and, subsequently, an executive of the Jewish Agency (the representative body of the Jews in Palestine) from 1935 to 1948. In this post he argued against Britain's mandates that limited Jewish immigration to Palestine. An ardent Zionist, he wanted Europe's Jews, who had been displaced by Nazi aggression during World War II, to have a place to resettle. After that war ended, Britain still refused to grant the Jews an independent homeland or to lift the immigration quotas. Ben-Gurion then sided with those Palestinian Jews who decided to take up arms against the British occupiers.

When Britain finally pulled out of Palestine, Ben-Gurion became Israel's first prime minister. He also took on the post of minister of defense and successfully beat back the Arab armies that invaded Israel when it declared statehood. Ben-Gurion held on to both positions from 1948 to 1963 (taking only a brief hiatus between 1953 and 1955). His popularity was immense, and with the backing of the people, Ben-Gurion created a thoroughly modern nation in only a few short years. He built industry, promoted education, established foreign trade, and most importantly, equipped and modernized Israel's army. Under constant threat by his Arab neighbors, Ben-Gurion kept the new nation alive. When Egypt tried to shut off vital shipping lanes by seizing the Suez Canal in 1956, Ben-Gurion launched an invasion of Egypt's Sinai Peninsula that captured the majority of the land right up to the banks of the Suez. The Israelis, though, later returned the Sinai under pressure from the international community.

Ben-Gurion resigned from office in 1963 after his fourth term as prime minister. A scandal had scarred his later years in office and split his Labor Party in two. He tried to run again in 1965 for prime minister under a new progressive party platform, but he was soundly beaten. He made one more showing in 1969, winning a

seat in the Israeli parliament. Lacking much political pull, he re-
tired to his retreat in the Negev Desert, where he helped found the
College of the Negev to encourage settlement in the area. Ben-
Gurion died in December 1973 from a brain hemorrhage.

Jimmy Carter

The son of a farmer and businessman, Jimmy Carter was born in
Plains, Georgia, in 1924 and spent his childhood there. At age nineteen, he enrolled in the U.S. Naval Academy at Annapolis, Maryland.
During his military service, he worked on the nation's earliest nuclear
submarines. He also met and married his wife, Rosalynn, while in the
navy. Though planning to continue his military career, Carter was
forced to leave the service when his father died in 1953. Carter and
his wife returned to Plains to manage the family business. For the
next several years, Carter balanced business and civic concerns and
became active in local politics. In 1962 he ran a race for the Georgia
Senate. His liberal views were not very popular, but Carter still won
his bid by the narrowest of margins. He earned a good reputation in
the state senate and was reelected for a second term. In 1966 Carter
set his sights on the governor's seat. He lost in the primaries, but his
faith and tenacity helped him run again in 1970. After an exhausting
campaign, Carter won the coveted office.

As governor, Carter focused on providing basic services and education to every citizen. He earned respect for decrying the racism
that kept many of Georgia's black population so impoverished. He
also helped bring more African Americans into government positions during his tenure in office. Carter saw opportunities in the
Democratic Party to extend his "fair treatment" policies to the rest
of the nation. While chairing the Democratic National Campaign
Committee in 1974, he announced that he would seek the presidential nomination in 1976. Despite being relatively unknown outside
Georgia, Carter pushed hard in his campaign and won the Democratic nomination. Vying against incumbent Gerald Ford for the
presidency, Carter promised to cut unemployment and help stir
business growth. Aided by strong support from blacks and working-
class whites, Carter won the election with ease.

The new president fought to end wasteful government spending
and to lower the federal income tax. His proposal to Congress to
establish a Department of Energy was also successfully adopted.
His record on internal affairs was marred, however, by high infla-
tion and a gasoline crisis. In foreign matters, Carter also had mixed

success. He won praise for using America's economic power to punish nations that routinely violated human rights. He also began the SALT II (Strategic Arms Limitation Talks) with the Soviet Union. And he successfully hosted and oversaw the signing of the 1978 Camp David Peace Accords between Israel and Egypt. But in 1979 Carter lost face when Iranian students took over the U.S. Embassy in Tehran and held fifty-two American embassy employees and visitors hostage. The Iranians wanted the deposed shah of Iran returned to their country in exchange for the hostages. The shah was undergoing medical treatment in America at the time, and Carter refused to hand him over to certain death. Carter tried economic sanctions and even a military rescue operation. Both failed, leaving the United States in a position of weakness. The hostages were finally released on Carter's last day as president, when it was already known that a new president, Ronald Reagan, was taking charge of America's destiny.

In his postpresidency, Jimmy Carter has worked tirelessly for humanitarian efforts both at home and abroad. He and his wife are involved with Habitat for Humanity, a nonprofit organization that builds housing for low-income families. He has also established the Carter Center which oversees elections in foreign countries and monitors human rights violations. Carter has also remained active as a goodwill diplomat for the United States, brokering many deals with antagonistic foreign leaders in the 1990s. Most recently, Carter has entered the fiction writers' market, publishing a novel in 2003 that takes place in revolutionary America.

Winston Churchill

Born in 1874, Winston Churchill was the son of Lord Randolph Churchill, a descendant of the seventh duke of Marlborough, and Jennie Jerome, the daughter of an American businessman. Neither of his parents was very attentive or caring, so young Churchill's home life was primarily unhappy. His tenure in school was also less than fulfilling. With no talent for most subjects, Churchill passed through without distinction. Fearing for his child's reputation (and his own), Winston's father pushed him into a military career. He was commissioned in the Fourth Hussars in 1895 and took part in campaigns in India and Sudan over the next four years. While enjoying the exploits of a soldier, Churchill also wrote newspaper accounts of his experiences. These accounts eventually were transformed into Churchill's first two published books. When he resigned his commission in 1899, Churchill banked on his journalistic skill and became a war correspondent, following the British army in the Boer War in South Africa. He was captured during the war but escaped from the prison camp where he was being held. He made his way back to England where he was celebrated both as a war hero and as the journalist who wrote about his own daring escape.

With a burgeoning reputation, Churchill turned to politics. He made a successful bid to enter the House of Commons in 1900 on the Conservative Party ticket. After a short time, however, his progressive ideals clashed with his party, and Churchill switched allegiance to the liberals. By the time of the First World War, Churchill had married and been appointed first lord of admiralty. Although he had the British navy in fighting trim by the onset of war, Churchill was demoted after casting his support for the disastrous Gallipoli campaign in Turkey. When David Lloyd George became prime minister in 1917, he instated Churchill as minister of munitions. And after the war, the energetic Churchill served as secretary of state for war and, later, colonial secretary.

In the 1920s Churchill returned to the Conservative Party and was appointed chancellor of exchequer in 1924 by Prime Minister Stanley Baldwin. He returned Britain to the gold standard and cracked down on labor unrest, two unpopular moves with the world edging closer to the economic depression of the early 1930s. But Churchill was out of office in 1929. He stayed in the public eye, however, warning against the growing threat of Nazi Germany. He was an outspoken critic of Prime Minister Neville Chamberlain's appeasement policy toward Germany, and his stance earned him a growing reputation—so much so that when war broke out in Europe, Chamberlain asked Churchill to resume his old position as lord of admiralty in 1939. Churchill accepted.

When the British people lost faith in Chamberlain's government, Churchill was named his successor in May 1940. Churchill realized Britain would have a tough time stemming the Nazi onslaught. Even as Britain stood alone fighting the Germans at the end of 1940, Churchill kept up the nation's morale with stirring speeches about the indomitable character of the Britons. When the United States entered the war in December 1941, Churchill gained a valuable ally in President Franklin Roosevelt. The two leaders cooperated in planning military strategy against Germany. With their countries united, the two men brought to bear the might and morale of the Western allies and crushed the Nazi war machine in western Europe. Their

Soviet ally, Joseph Stalin, had done likewise in eastern Europe, but his plan was to keep the territory he had conquered and transform it into satellite nations for Communist Russia. Churchill, though thankful for the Russian zeal in defeating Nazism, feared the former ally would become the next grave threat to democracy.

In 1945, with the Second World War at an end, Churchill warned Roosevelt and Britain's government of the dangers of Soviet Russia. Neither Roosevelt nor the war-weary British were inclined to heed his cautions. That year, the tenure of the Conservatives and Churchill were at an end. The Labour Party formed the new government. From 1945 to 1951, Churchill, having won a seat in the House of Commons, led the opposition in Parliament. One of the concerns he focused on was British policy toward Palestine. Fearing a quagmire that would further drain the nation's military and economic resources, Churchill argued for Britain to pull out of the region. The nation seemed to agree, and Churchill's reputation remained strong. In 1951, at age seventy-six, he was appointed prime minister for a second time when the Conservatives returned to power. Churchill held Britain together through the early years of the Cold War, showing the nation's resolve to stand by the United States against any Soviet menace. In 1953 he was knighted for his contributions to the empire; two years later he stepped down as prime minister and went back to serving in the House of Commons. It was a position he held until his death on January 24, 1965.

Abba Eban

Abba Eban was born in Capetown, South Africa, in 1915. His parents moved to Britain when he was young, and there Eban excelled in academic studies. When World War II erupted, Eban volunteered for the British army and eventually attained the rank of major. An avid Zionist, Eban spent much of his military service in the Middle East. At one point he was Britain's liaison officer with the Jewish Agency, the Jewish representative body in Palestine before Israel declared statehood. After the war, he remained with the Jewish Agency, becoming one of its representatives to the United Nations. Eban was one of the chief spokesmen who petitioned the United Nations to partition Palestine into Jewish and Arab states.

When Israel declared its statehood in 1948, Eban continued his work in the United Nations as the new nation's permanent representative—a post he held from 1949 to 1959. At the same time, Eban served as Israel's ambassador to the United States. The dual role made him a recognizable figure, one who came to represent Israel's initial struggle to survive through the conflicts that defined the first decade of Israel's existence. In 1959 Eban left the United Nations and took up a position in the Knesset, Israel's parliament. As a member of the Labor Party, he earned two ministerial positions over the following four years. While serving as minister of education and culture between 1959 and 1963, Eban was responsible for encouraging Jews in Asia and Africa to immigrate to Israel.

In 1963, when Levi Eshkol became prime minister of Israel, Eban was appointed his deputy prime minister until 1966. In that year he was made foreign minister because of his adroit and passionate oratory and his past experiences as a representative of Israel. Both served him well in the international community as Israel fought the Six-Day War in 1967 and the Yom Kippur War in 1973. Always appearing ready to compromise while at the same time defending Israeli interests, Eban was instrumental in negotiating the return of the Sinai Peninsula and the Golan Heights (to Egypt and Syria, repectively) after Israeli forces seized them in the Yom Kippur War. Eban believed that keeping too much Arab land would characterize Israel as a conqueror rather than a peaceful nation with a right to its own security. Even when he left the Israeli cabinet in 1974 and returned to his seat in the Knesset, Eban continued to voice his concern that occupying Arab land—such as the West Bank territories—would weaken Israel's claim to be a legitimate Jewish state.

While serving in the Knesset, Eban turned out several published works on Israel's history and on world affairs. In 1984, when the Labor Party once more took power, he was appointed chairman of the parliamentary committee on foreign and security affairs. It was another position in which he could use his considerable talents in moderating the government's relations with Israel's Arab neighbors. Eban remained in the Knesset until 1988. But even in retirement, he remained a political force. In his declining years, he continued to publish books on Israel and politics. He died in his adopted homeland in 2002.

Dwight D. Eisenhower

The man who would become the thirty-fourth president of the United States was born in Denison, Texas, in 1890. His family moved later to Abilene, Kansas, where his father took a job in a creamery. The Eisenhowers were very poor, which forced upon

Dwight and his five brothers a sense of thrift and self-reliance. His mother and father also valued education, and Dwight became a good student, favoring history above other subjects. Young Eisenhower was also a gifted athlete and enjoyed the rugged outdoor life offered in rural Abilene. With his academic talent and his physical fitness, Eisenhower entered West Point Military Academy in 1911 to attain a college education at the government's expense.

Graduating from West Point in 1915, Eisenhower had become an army officer who believed in serving his country. He married his wife Mamie in 1916, while Europe was embroiled in the First World War. When America entered the war in 1917, Eisenhower ached for a combat command. His talents for organization and training soldiers, however, kept him stateside for many months. In October 1918 he finally received orders to go to the front lines in France, but within a month the war ended without Eisenhower having any battlefield experience. Between 1920 and 1936 Eisenhower received and kept the rank of major in the army. The interwar years were uneventful for Eisenhower. In 1926 he graduated first in his class from the army's Command and General Staff School and served as a staff officer to many prominent military figures in the American army. His success as a staff officer, though, kept him out of any potential battlefield commands. Finally in 1940 Eisenhower was made a colonel, and on the eve of America's entrance into the Second World War, he became a general in September 1941.

Eisenhower's rise during World War II was remarkable. Initially he served as an adviser to the army chief of staff, General George Marshall, briefing him on the situation in the Pacific. Marshall recognized the talents and commitment of his aide and sent him to England in 1942 to discuss plans with the British about a possible invasion of Nazi-held Europe. The precursor to the large-scale invasion of Europe was Operation Torch, the U.S. beach landings in North Africa in November 1942. Eisenhower was put in charge of this invasion, which was designed to test him and the relatively inexperienced American army. Eisenhower passed the test, though it was a challenge fraught with many mistakes. During the subsequent invasions of Sicily and Italy, Eisenhower had more experience and confidence. And by the time he was given command of the Normandy invasion in June 1944, he was a four-star general.

The Anglo-American beach landings in Normandy, France, hastened the end of the war in western Europe. Eisenhower followed the progress of the army from Normandy to Paris and eventually across the Rhine into Germany. His reputation among Allied leaders was considerable, and his popularity at home was growing. At war's end, many politicians—both Democrat and Republican—made overtures to get the war hero to run for president. Eisenhower refused. He did, however, retire from the army in 1948 and accept the presidency of Columbia University in New York. Three years later he was recalled to active duty. This time he was to serve as the supreme commander of the armed forces of the North Atlantic Treaty Organization (NATO). He kept the position for only a year. By that time he had been hounded by the Republican Party to run for president of the United States. Believing the American people were calling him to duty, Eisenhower gave in and accepted the nomination in 1952. His immense popularity assured his victory.

As president, Eisenhower was a moderate conservative. He did nothing to upset any past laws or governmental projects; instead, he focused on keeping the country financially sound. Not willing to increase spending even on the military, Eisenhower supported the U.S. commitment to nuclear weapons as the cheap deterrent. He also sought to open negotiations with the Soviet Union to decrease tensions between America and its new Cold War enemy. Eisenhower's presidency was marked by many other foreign policy matters, including ending the war in Korea in 1953. His approach to all foreign policies seemed to emphasize moderation and America's support for the strict adherence to international law.

In 1960 Eisenhower had completed a second term as president. Rather thankful that he could not resume office for a third time, Eisenhower gave a farewell speech that bespoke his respect for the position while warning future presidents of a "military-industrial complex" that was rapidly gaining influence over national policy making. After exiting office, Eisenhower and his wife retired to their farm in Gettysburg, Pennsylvania. There he began writing his memoirs, which would be later prepared for publication by his son. Dwight David Eisenhower died on March 28, 1969. He was buried in Abilene on the grounds of the library and museum that bear his name.

Levi Eshkol

Born Levi Shkolnik in the Ukraine in 1895, Eshkol was educated by a rabbi in his early years. He then went to Hebrew school in Lithuania where he stayed until he was nineteen. A committed

Zionist, Eshkol then moved to Palestine in 1914 to work on building the first Jewish kibbutzim, or settlements, in the region. In 1920 Eshkol helped found a labor organization called the Histadrut. With labor leanings, he soon joined the Labor Party in the Jewish Agency (the Jewish representative body in Palestine before Israel declared statehood). Eshkol worked to build and promote kibbutzim through the 1920s. He married Elisheva Kaplan in 1928 (it was Eshkol's second marriage; his first had ended in divorce).

Eshkol spent the 1930s in Germany as the shadow of Adolf Hitler's Nazi state threatened European Jewry. His mission was to convince German Jews of the coming danger and help them resettle in Palestine. By the time the Second World War broke out, Eshkol was back in Palestine. In 1948, when Israel declared its statehood, Levi Shkolnik officially took on the Hebraic variant of his name, Eshkol. Under the new government, Eshkol was appointed director general of the ministry of defense. He held the position until 1951, when he became minister of agriculture and development, and the following year he was made minister of finance.

With success as a finance minister, Eshkol was appointed prime minister when the post was vacated by David Ben-Gurion in 1963. Upon receiving the appointment, Eshkol resigned from the financial ministry but took on the post of defense minister. He held both positions through his term as prime minister. In 1965 Ben-Gurion made a second bid for the prime minister's seat, but Eshkol held out in the elections. His second term, however, was marred by a perceived weakness in handling Israel's Arab neighbors. In 1967, when Egyptian president Nasser closed the Gulf of Aqaba (the shipping route that brought Israel the bulk of its imports), many Israelis clamored for war. Eshkol, however, wanted to resolve the matter diplomatically. Unable to achieve any headway, he lost his position as defense minister to Moshe Dayan, a hard-nosed "hawk" who became the hero of the Six-Day War. Eshkol lived out his few remaining years with his third wife Miriam (whom he married in 1964, five years after his second wife had died). His life and tenure as prime minister ended in 1969 when he died of a heart attack in Jerusalem.

King Hussein I

Hussein ibn Talal was born in Amman, Jordan, in 1935. He was a member of the royal Hashemite family that includes in its lineage the prophet Muhammad. Hussein's grandfather, King Abdullah, was the founder of modern Jordan. When Abdullah was assassinated in 1951, Hussein's father inherited the throne. Hussein's father, however, suffered from mental illness, and within a year the Jordanian parliament voted to have him removed as king. Then in 1953 the eighteen-year-old Hussein ibn Talal became King Hussein I.

The kingdom that Hussein inherited was extremely impoverished. It was facing incursions from Israel in the West Bank settlements along the Jordan River, and Arab nationalism in the region was calling upon Jordan to stand against the upstart Israel. Although Hussein was no friend to the Israelis, he was more concerned with strengthening his nation's economy than fighting expensive conflicts. Still, in 1967 Jordan joined forces with the Syrians and Egyptians to invade Israel. The resulting Six-Day War was a disaster for the Arab coalition, and Jordan lost the West Bank territory to the Israelis. The loss of the West Bank, which was inhabited mainly by Palestinians, prompted the Palestinian guerrilla war. The Palestinians first targeted Israel for its occupation of the region, but by 1970 the guerrillas also began attacking Jordan for trying to rid Jordanian territory of secret Palestinian training camps. At the same time it was contending with the Palestinians, Jordan was threatened by an invasion from Syria. King Hussein led the strong Jordanian army through both struggles, but the death and destruction within Jordan was great. During the next three years all that Hussein had done to help the Jordanian economy was ruined by the fighting.

In the late 1970s Jordan's economy was stimulated by an oil boom. Hussein aided the nation's prosperity by allowing greater economic freedom to its citizens. The newfound wealth helped Jordan rebuild, but when oil prices fell in the mid-1980s the economy slowed again. Hussein spent much of the new decade trying to broker Palestinian-Israeli peace initiatives laid out by American president Ronald Reagan. This diplomatic mission, coupled with his past run-ins with his Arab neighbors, gave Western leaders the impression that Hussein was a useful ally in the Middle East. This changed, however, in 1991 when an American-led coalition challenged Iraq's Saddam Hussein. Iraq had been Jordan's principal trade partner, and though initially declaring neutrality, King Hussein eventually sided with Saddam Hussein. This decision made many Westerners wary of Jordan's questionable allegiances.

Regardless of his foreign alliances, King Hussein was still deeply committed to modernizing and stabilizing (though many Arab nations interpreted it as Westernizing) Jordan from within. He reinstated multiparty elections—something which had not occurred in Jordan since 1956. He also threw his support behind the plan to offer Palestinians self-rule in some of the Israeli-occupied territories. He had already recognized the Palestine Liberation Organization as a legitimate government; he then decided in 1994 to officially end the state of war that had existed between Jordan and Israel for more than two decades. The United States (which had been a source of foreign aid since the 1950s) greeted this latter act with approval and, due to Hussein's commitment to peace, canceled Jordan's remaining debt. In 1998 King Hussein flew to America, though not on a goodwill visit. Instead, he was checked into the Mayo Clinic to undergo treatment for cancer. It was a battle he did not win. He died in 1999 and was succeeded by his son, Crown Prince Abdullah.

Abu Mazen

Abu Mazen was born Mahmoud Abbas in British-controlled Palestine in 1935. In 1948, when Israel's independence was challenged by an Arab invasion, he and his family relocated to Syria. He earned a law degree from the University of Damascus and furthered his education in Moscow. Along with his friend Yasser Arafat, Abbas was a founding member of al-Fatah ("armed struggle"), a political organization set up in the late 1950s to promote Palestinian liberation. He then became widely known as Abu Mazen. When Arafat got control of the Palestine Liberation Organization (PLO) in 1969, Mazen followed him into the organization as a major organizer and fundraiser. Mazen, however, was more moderate than many of his colleagues and became known for his willingness to negotiate with the Israelis. In 1980 Mazen was chosen to lead the PLO's department for national and international relations. He also joined the executive committee of the PLO as secretary general.

When Arafat was shut out of the Palestinian-Israeli peace talks in 2003 for not doing enough to end Palestinian terrorism, Arafat appointed Mazen as the new prime minister of the recently inaugurated Palestinian state. It was an awkward position for Mazen since he had not been popularly elected to the post and seemed merely a puppet of Arafat's making. But Mazen proved his strength by not kowtowing to Arafat's demands. He began dealing with hawkish Israeli prime minister Ariel Sharon to carry the peace plan forward, and many Western leaders saw Mazen as a potentially stabilizing force in the region. However, as soon as talks began, Palestinian militants carried out suicide bombings that appeared to undercut Palestine's commitment to peace. It was clear that Mazen did not have the power to curtail the dedicated militant forces still opposed to Israel's existence. Mazen resigned his post in September 2003.

Golda Meir

Golda Meir was born Goldie Mabovitch in the Ukraine in 1898. Her family immigrated to the United States in 1906 and settled in Milwaukee, Wisconsin. There, she attended a teachers' college in 1917, the same year she married Morris Myerson (whose name she later shortened to Meir). She taught in the schools in the Milwaukee region for the next four years and became active in the Zionist movement. In 1921 the Myersons left the United States to settle in British-controlled Palestine. They spent some time on a kibbutz, but Morris, displeased with that lifestyle, forced the couple to relocate to Jerusalem. Meir became a housewife and mother of two in Jerusalem, but she was still committed to building settlements and realizing the Zionist dream of a Jewish homeland. She shuttled between Jerusalem and her old kibbutz to satisfy her desire to promote Zionism.

In 1928 Meir joined the Histadrut, the Jewish workers' union, and agreed to travel to England to raise money and encourage settlement of Palestine. She left her family behind for a short time; then when her daughter Sarah got sick, she took the children to New York, where Sarah could receive medical care. In New York, Meir worked with the Pioneer Women, an American organization of Jewish women committed to Zionism. In 1929, after her daughter's recovery, Meir returned to Palestine and her husband. Because of her greater devotion to Zionism than to Morris, Meir and her husband agreed to separate (unofficially) and live apart, though Morris remained a constant visitor in Meir's new home.

By 1935 Meir had worked her way up the ladder of command in the Histadrut. She held executive positions in the organization for the next few years as the Second World War loomed in Europe and more and more Jews fled Nazi persecution. In 1942, when the British limited Jewish immigration to Palestine, Meir was among the vocal protesters. She and her children also took part in smuggling Jews into the country to evade the British quotas. She became the head of the Jewish Agency, the governing organization that represented the Jews to their British rulers, when its former leader David Ben-Gurion was jailed for his defiance of the British laws.

After the war it became clear that England, bowing to international pressure and its own weariness, would allow the Jews in Palestine to form their own independent state. With this prospect would certainly come an attack by the new nation's Arab neighbors who believed the Jews had no right to Palestinian land. Meir was, therefore, selected to travel to America to raise funds for the defense of the Jewish homeland. She was extremely successful in this mission, raising more than $50 million. She returned to Palestine in time to take part in the official ceremonies that inaugurated the new nation of Israel. But within hours of its declaration of statehood, the new nation was attacked by an Arab coalition led by Egypt, Jordan, and Syria. Meir was sent back to the United States to raise more funds. While there, she received a cable from Israel, asking her to become the ambassador to the Soviet Union. She agreed, and with her daughter, she went to Moscow in 1948.

Israel won its war for independence in 1949, and Meir returned to Israel to take up a position in the new Israeli parliament, the Knesset. David Ben-Gurion had been elected Israel's first prime minister, and he chose Meir to take a seat in his cabinet as minister of labor. She worked relentlessly to build housing for the millions of displaced Jews who had come to Israel since the beginning of World War II. Ben-Gurion praised her efforts and in 1956 appointed her foreign minister, the second most powerful position in the government. It was then, under Ben-Gurion's urging, that she hebraized her name to Meir. Throughout Ben-Gurion's tenure, Meir served her government faithfully. In 1965, though, she decided it was time to retire. She was suffering from ill health and had been hospitalized several times over her career. Her retirement, however, lasted only a month. She agreed to return to politics as secretary general of the Workers' Party.

In 1967 Israel fought the Six-Day War. In January of the following year, the new Israel Labor Party was founded and Meir was elected secretary general. At age seventy, after six months in her new position, she again announced retirement. This time her retirement lasted eight months. In February 1969 Prime Minister Levi Eshkol died of a heart attack while in office. The Labor Party chose to name Meir as his successor until later elections could be held. What was meant to be a nine-month stint turned into a four-year job as the elections reinstated the Labor government with Meir as prime minister.

With failing health but intense resolve, Meir held the reins of government firm. The United Nations had brokered the cease-fire that ended the Six-Day War, but Meir's administration agreed to open peace talks in hopes of ending all hostility with Israel's neighbors. The peace did not last, however, as the Arabs again attacked Israel during the Yom Kippur War in 1973. Even though Israel successfully defended itself, the nation was caught unprepared, and Meir's government took the blame. In 1974 she resigned and finally retired. She spent her remaining years with her children and her grandchildren. She died in 1978, a beloved figure to Israelis.

Gamal Abdel Nasser

Gamal Abdel Nasser was born in Alexandria, Egypt, in 1918, when Britain controlled Egypt as a protectorate. Resistance to British rule was strong in the 1920s and 1930s, and Nasser grew up in this period of intense nationalism and instability. At age nineteen, he began his long military career. Nasser entered the military academy in Cairo and graduated the following year as a second lieutenant. In 1943, after serving both at home and in Sudan, Nasser returned to Cairo and took up an instructor position at the military academy, later transferring to the army staff college. In 1948, when Egypt joined a coalition of Arab states that invaded the new nation of Israel, Nasser, now a major, commanded three Egyptian tank battalions surrounded by an Israeli force just southwest of Jerusalem. He held off repeated attacks until the Arabs sued for peace within a few months of the war's beginning.

Humiliated by the defeat, many young Egyptian military officers—Nasser among them—blamed the increasingly despotic government of King Farouk, which also happened to be tolerant of the British presence in Egypt. This organization of disaffected military men, called the Free Officers Movement, overthrew the king in 1952. Nasser then became one of the executive staff of the new government. In two years Nasser ousted the ruling general and took on the title of prime minister. In 1956 he was elected the first president of the Egyptian Republic. He disbanded the monarchy and purged the nation of lingering British influence, filling vacated government and civil service positions with Egyptians.

Initially, Nasser's new government tried to work with Western leaders, but the West—especially the United States—was unwilling to trade arms to Egypt because of its anti-Israel stance. He turned to the Soviet bloc to attain weapons, another move that alienated the West. Then in 1956 he nationalized the Suez Canal, which still had been under the control of England and France only two years before. In a show of power, the French and British—along with the Israelis—tried to retake the canal but eventually bowed to international pressure to relinquish the region forever. Nasser subsequently moved Egypt toward neutrality in the growing Cold War. He accepted help from any nation that offered, but he did not respond with any pledge of allegiance to the donor. His main concern was to build industry and national defense to make Egypt one of the more advanced nations in Africa.

In 1958 Nasser presided over the union of Syria and Egypt into the United Arab Republic. The union was short-lived, however, as Syria withdrew three years later. Nasser then began instituting some Socialist polices such as agrarian reform and industrial mobilization. During the following years, he enjoyed immense popularity as a military man who could still attend to the needs of the nation. In 1967, however, Nasser's powerful military suffered a stinging defeat during the Six-Day War, when Israel launched a surprise attack on Egypt and surrounded and destroyed large elements of the Egyptian army and air force. Nasser offered to resign under the shadow of humiliation, but the nation stood behind him and kept him in office. Wanting to channel more of Egypt's finances into social projects, Nasser tentatively accepted an American plan to broker peace between the Arab states and Israel after the war. Unfortunately, he died in 1970 before any solid peace could be established.

Yitzhak Rabin

Yitzhak Rabin was born in Jerusalem in 1922 when Britain controlled Palestine. He joined the Palmach, an elite Jewish defense force in 1940. After World War II Rabin and the Palmach turned their attention to ridding Palestine of the British. In 1948, when the British vacated the region and Arab armies tried to destroy the newly established nation of Israel, Rabin commanded a Palmach brigade that helped break the siege of Jerusalem. For his conduct and experience, Rabin then rose through the ranks of the Israel Defense Force (IDF), the new nation's military. In 1964 he was appointed chief of staff of the IDF and, three years later, headed the Israeli military in the Six-Day War against Egypt, Jordan, and Syria.

In 1968 Rabin left the military to become Israel's ambassador to the United States. He served at this post until 1973, when he returned to Israel and joined the Labor Party. In that year he was elected to the Knesset, the Israeli parliament. A year later he became the minister of labor in the cabinet of Prime Minister Golda Meir. When Meir resigned in 1974 because of protests over her handling of the Yom Kippur War of the previous year, Rabin was chosen to succeed her. Rabin headed the state until 1977 when elections removed the Labor Party from power. He spent the next few years leading the opposition party in the Knesset, and in 1984 he rejoined the cabinet as minister of defense under a coalition government. He served with that government until 1990. Then, in 1992 he ran for prime minister again under a coalition platform dedicated to thoroughly restructuring Israel's foreign and domestic policies. He won the election after asking Israeli voters to cast their ballots for him as an individual rather than for his coalition party.

The new Rabin government inherited the slow progress of the Arab-Israeli peace talks begun a year before Rabin took office. The previous conservative government had jeopardized the talks by insisting on Israel's right to build Jewish settlements in the West Bank and the Gaza Strip, two disputed regions where Palestinian Arabs lived. In an unpredicted move, Rabin called for the cessation of settlement. He allowed the Palestinians in these regions to establish an autonomous government under Palestine Liberation Organization leader Yasser Arafat. In 1994 Rabin, Arafat, and Israeli foreign minister Shimon Peres shared the Nobel Peace Prize for their efforts in advancing peace in the region. The dream of ultimate and lasting peace, however, was never achieved in Rabin's lifetime. He was assassinated in 1995 by a right-wing Jewish extremist who believed Rabin had sold the Jews out to the Arabs.

Anwar el-Sadat

Anwar el-Sadat was born in an Egyptian village just north of Cairo in 1918. He spent seven years in the care of his grandmother while his parents were in the Sudan (where his father was working). Sadat's parents returned in 1925, and young Anwar went to live with them in Cairo. As he grew, he took part in demonstrations against the British, who were in control of Egypt at the time. In 1936 he entered the Cairo military academy. He graduated in 1938 and was posted in Manqabad in Upper Egypt. There he met Gamal Abdel Nasser, another graduate of the academy who, like Sadat, hoped to see Egypt rid of the British.

While Nasser spent the years of World War II posted in Sudan, Sadat remained in Egypt, plotting against the British. He was arrested in 1942 for aiding German spies. He spent two years in jail before he escaped. He lived out the rest of the war in hiding. In 1946 he was again arrested for playing a part in the assassination of a pro-British Egyptian minister, Amin Osama. After a long-delayed trial, he was released in 1948 for lack of evidence. At that time Israel had declared statehood and the Egyptian army took part in an Arab invasion of the fledgling nation. Sadat had no part in the attack since he had been suspended from the military during his trial. He was reinstated as a captain, however, in 1950. He then met up with his old friend Nasser who had fallen in with the Free Officers Movement, an organization devoted to disposing of the current anglophile government and nationalizing the country. With popular support, the Free Officers staged a coup and sent King Farouk into exile in 1952. Nasser eventually gained control of Egypt in 1954, and over the next fifteen years, he saddled Sadat with a variety of minor governmental posts. Sadat was very loyal to Nasser, a trait that eventually earned him the vice presidency in 1969 when Nasser's rule was coming to an end.

In 1970 Nasser died of a heart attack. Sadat was appointed his successor. Sadat's relationship to Nasser made his position unstable. The opposition party had grown powerful and even some members of the military assumed he could easily be removed from office. But Sadat preempted any coup by staging a "Corrective Revolution" in 1971 that purged the government of his enemies. Now with the solid backing of the army, Sadat began instituting his policies. He organized a pact with Syria to launch a surprise invasion of Israeli-held territory in 1973. Sadat aimed at recapturing the Sinai Penin-sula, which the Israelis had previously taken from Egypt. The re-sulting Yom Kippur War caught the Israelis off guard, but they were quick to rally and defeat the Arab coalition. American diplomacy eventually secured an Israeli withdrawal from parts of the Sinai, and Egypt decided to cast Egypt as a friend to the United States. In 1977 Sadat tried to show the West his willingness to move away from fur-ther Arab coalitions by visiting Israel on a goodwill tour. In the fol-lowing year Sadat and Israeli prime minister Menachem Begin signed the Camp David Peace Accords under U.S. auspices, and in 1979 they concluded a final peace agreement. Sadat and Begin shared the 1978 Nobel Peace Prize for their efforts.

While the peace process went forward, Sadat continued casting Egypt as an independent entity and not part of a greater Arab con-federation. The Arab states that had approved of Nasser's commit-ment to pan-Arab brotherhood were angered by Sadat's disloyalty.

Most other Arab nations who were part of the Arab League pulled their ambassadors from Egypt and moved the headquarters of the league from Cairo to Tunis. The United States, not unexpectedly, was pleased by Sadat's apparent defection. It courted the Egyptian leader with massive financial aid. Quickly, Sadat Westernized Egypt, embracing a free market economy and turning some nationalized industries back to private ownership. The new liberalized economy had a downside, however. The money made from imports and tourism went into the pockets of a select few. A minority of industrial leaders got rich, but the average worker saw little benefits of the new system. In 1977 workers and students rioted, but the army remained loyal to Sadat and put down the unrest.

It was not only Sadat's policies that angered many Egyptians; it was also his extravagant lifestyle. Both he and his second wife, who was half-British, adopted a Westernized image that did not sit well with the people. Fundamentalist elements painted Sadat's government as tainted and corrupt, and membership in the more extreme organizations grew. On October 6, 1981, Muslim radicals gunned Sadat down while he was reviewing a military parade. While millions of Egyptian mourners had taken to the streets when Gamal Nasser died, few ventured out to pay tribute to Anwar el-Sadat.

Ariel Sharon

Ariel Sharon was born in February 1928 near Tel Aviv, in what was then British-controlled Palestine. Sharon became active in military exploits quite early. At age fourteen, he was involved with the Jewish underground defense force that protected Jewish settlements from Arabs. Six years later, when the nation of Israel declared its independence in the region, Sharon commanded an infantry platoon against the pan-Arab coalition that sought to destroy the new Jewish homeland. It was then that Sharon was wounded in the battle for Jerusalem. In 1951–1952 he served as an intelligence officer, and in 1953 he founded Commando Unit 101, which struck back at Palestinian terrorist groups. Between 1958 and 1962, Sharon ran the Infantry Corps School because of his experience and dedication to Israel's defense. He was later appointed head of all army training activities. During the 1967 Six-Day War, Sharon received a frontline command as a major general. He adeptly led an armored division against the Egyptian army in the Sinai desert. After that challenge, Sharon was given the rank of brigadier general and sent to the Gaza Strip to suppress Palestinian terrorism.

Sharon left the army in July 1973 and cast his lot with politics. His new career was briefly interrupted in October when Egyptian and Syrian armies invaded during the Yom Kippur War. Sharon was temporarily called upon to lead a reserve unit to halt the Egyptian advance in the Sinai. When the conflict ended, he returned to politics and won a seat in the Knesset, the Israeli parliament. His tenure was brief, and he resigned within a year. In 1975 Prime Minister Yitzhak Rabin made Sharon an adviser on security matters. Sharon had talent for the post, but he was not content with the Rabin administration's waffling stance on Jewish settlement of the occupied Palestinian territories of Gaza and the West Bank. Sharon quit the government in 1976 to form the Shlomtzion Party, which was devoted to maintaining the Jewish settlements. The Shlomtzion did not fare well in the 1977 elections, so Sharon opted to merge his party with the victorious Likud Party. In that year the Likud had installed Menachem Begin as prime minister, and Begin appointed Sharon to his cabinet. As minister of agriculture, Sharon continued to promote settlement of the occupied territories.

In 1981 Begin made Sharon the minister of defense. In this position he stepped up Israeli military presence in the occupied territories to counteract the momentum of the Palestine Liberation Organization (PLO). He also became involved in—if not directly designed—Israel's military strikes against suspected PLO targets in Lebanon in 1982. Though harshly criticized for his part in the attacks (which Israel did not call off until 1985), Sharon kept defending his actions with tenacity. When Shimon Peres became prime minister after Begin's resignation in 1983, Sharon was soon brought into the new government as minister of industry.

In the 1990s, when Israel and Palestine were trying to establish a peaceful coexistence, Sharon remained active in politics. In 1998, under the administration of Benjamin Netanyahu, Sharon was made foreign minister. Although Palestinians feared that Sharon would take a hard line in the peace negotiations between Israel and the PLO, Sharon proved willing to talk and listen. He was instrumental in hammering out the initial agreements between Israel and the new Palestinian Authority, the autonomous government in Palestine that was inaugurated with Israel's permission. In 1999, when Labor Party candidate Ehud Barak succeeded Netanyahu as prime minister, Sharon took over the Likud Party, the current party of opposition. Barak resigned in 2000, and Sharon won a special prime ministerial election by a large margin of parliamentary votes.

As prime minister, Sharon asserted that he was in favor of peace between Arabs and Jews in Palestine, but his proposed peace plan involved the unrealistic demilitarization of Palestine. With no Palestinians willing to give up their weapons, Sharon relied on the Israeli military to keep the peace—an unpopular move with Arabs and the West. In 2003, when Israel held its first popular elections, Sharon won a second term as prime minister. Under pressure from the United States, Sharon agreed to a reinvigorated plan for peace that calls for the creation of a separate Palestinian state and the removal of specific Jewish settlements in the occupied territories. But with America's attention diverted by war in Iraq and its war on terror, the plan has not been implemented and Sharon has felt no compulsion to adhere to its strictures.

George J. Tomeh

George J. Tomeh was Syria's permanent representative in the United Nations General Assembly. He was later made an adviser to the Institute for Palestine Studies. Tomeh has also brought together all the UN resolutions relevant to the Palestine question and the Arab-Israeli conflict from 1947 to 1998 in a five-volume work called *United Nations Resolutions on Palestine and the Arab-Israeli Conflict*.

Chronology

1878
Jews erect the first Zionist settlement in Palestine.

1896
Theodor Herzl publishes *The Jewish State*, a work that promotes Zionism, the belief that the Jews should return to the Holy Land to build a Jewish state.

1897
The First Zionist Congress convenes in Switzerland to discuss creating a Jewish homeland in Palestine.

1916
May 9: England and France conclude the Sykes-Picot Agreement that divides up portions of the Middle East into British and French zones of influence. Britain attains control of Palestine.

1917
November 2: The British issue the Balfour Declaration which implies that Britain favors an independent Jewish homeland in Palestine.

1918
November: After World War I ends, Muslims and Christians in Jerusalem form an association to oppose a Jewish homeland in Palestine.

1919
August 28: Submitting its report to President Woodrow Wilson, a U.S. commission of inquiry argues against supporting a potential Jewish homeland in Palestine.

1920
February: Arabs launch the first attacks against Jewish settlements in Palestine.

June: The Jews organize Haganah, a self-defense organization designed to protect settlements.

1922
March: Britain grants independence to Egypt.

July 24: The British Mandate for Palestine creates Transjordan as a separate state.

1929
August: Arabs riot in several Palestinian cities; in Hebron, more than sixty Jews are killed in the rioting; in Jerusalem, thousands of Jews flee the city in fear of their lives.

1930
October 21: The British White Paper limits further Jewish immigration to Palestine.

1936–1939
The first major Arab revolt claims the lives of hundreds of Jews; the British military puts down the revolt, killing thousands of Arabs.

1939
November: A second British White Paper is issued; it sets Jewish immigration cap to seventy-five thousand and speaks of a Palestinian state controlled by the Arabs.

1945
March: As World War II draws to a close, Egypt, Iraq, Lebanon, Saudi Arabia, Syria, Transjordan, and Yemen unite as the League of Arab States; the organization works with England to gradually shift the burden of Middle East management to Arabs.

1947
July 18: A British naval vessel rams the *Exodus*, a cargo ship

loaded with illegal Jewish immigrants headed for Palestine; the damaged vessel is towed to Haifa, but the passengers are eventually sent back to Germany; the incident focuses world-wide criticism upon the British government and promotes sympathy for the Zionist cause.

November 29: UN Resolution 181 calls for the partition of Palestine into Jewish and Palestinian states; the Arabs in the region and in neighboring states refuse to recognize the resolution.

1948
May 15: The British abandon Palestine; the Jews immediately declare the independence of the state of Israel, which triggers an invasion by Egypt, Jordan, Iraq, Saudi Arabia, and Syria.

1949
June: Arabs and Jews conclude an armistice, after the Israelis succeed in capturing 50 percent more land than was allotted to them by the UN partition plan.

1951
July: King Abdullah of Jordan is assassinated; his son, Hussein I, succeeds to the throne.

1952
July: A military coup ousts King Farouk of Egypt for his tolerance of British influence in Egyptian affairs; Gamal Abdel Nasser eventually takes control of the country.

1955
Israel and Egypt fight skirmishes across the Gaza demilitarized zone; Israel also launches a retaliatory invasion against Syria following an attack on an Israeli patrol boat.

1956
July: Nasser nationalizes the Suez Canal, provoking immediate military retaliation from England and France; the British and French governments work in collaboration with Israel.

October 29: Because of escalating border conflicts, Israel seizes the Sinai Peninsula from Egypt, thus occupying lands up to the Suez Canal. The Israelis returned the land due to mounting international criticism.

1957

Yasser Arafat is among Palestinian activists who form al-Fatah, an organization dedicated to liberating Palestine by destroying Israel.

1964

May: With support from Egypt, the Palestine Liberation Organization (PLO) is founded to manage Palestinian freedom-fighting efforts.

September 13: Arab nations in the Middle East hold a second Arab summit in Alexandria, Egypt; one resolution of the convention is a pledge to work toward the destruction of Israel.

1967

May: Nasser closes the Strait of Tiran to Israeli shipping.

June 6–11: Israel launches the Six-Day War against its Arab neighbors; the Israelis seize the Gaza Strip and Sinai from Egypt, the West Bank from Jordan, and the Golan Heights from Syria.

November: Under pressure from the United Nations, the Israelis return parts of the conquered regions.

1967–1968

Israel stages several raids into the West Bank to eliminate PLO and al-Fatah bases; the Jordanian military steps in to repulse the attacks.

1969

February: Arafat takes over the PLO leadership and heads the Palestine National Council (PNC), which declares its intentions to create a democratic state for Muslims, Christians, and Jews.

1970

September: King Hussein of Jordan moves against the PLO to clear Jordanian land of this constant source of Israeli provocation; the PLO relocates in Lebanon; Nasser dies and Anwar el-Sadat becomes head of the Egyptian state.

1973

October 6: During the Jewish holiday of Yom Kippur, Egypt and Syria launch a successful surprise attack to retake the Suez Canal region and the Golan Heights; the Israeli army regroups and strikes back, nullifying the Arab gains.

October 22: The United Nations compels Israel to return the Sinai to Egypt and cede part of the Golan Heights back to Syria.

1974

November 13: Arafat addresses the United Nations, symbolically carrying a gun and an olive branch; he indicates the PLO will accept peace or further warfare depending on how the United Nations regards Palestinian independence; the United Nations decides to recognize the Palestinian right to sovereignty but does not indicate that a separate Palestinian state is currently feasible.

1977

June 20: The conservative Likud Party takes power in Israel with Menachem Begin as prime minister; the Likud authorizes increased Jewish settlement in the occupied parts of the West Bank and Gaza Strip.

November 20: Sadat visits Israel and speaks before the Knesset; he argues for a Palestinian state but also offers peace between Egypt and Israel.

1978

March 15: In retaliation for PLO attacks, Israel invades Lebanon; the United Nations calls for an immediate Israeli withdrawal; the Israelis do not comply with the full terms of the United Nations' request until May 2000.

1979
March 26: After holding meetings together in the United States in September 1978, Menachem Begin and Anwar el-Sadat conclude a peace treaty between Israel and Egypt.

1981
October 6: Sadat is assassinated by Egyptian extremists.

1982
Israel invades Lebanon again; Lebanese fundamentalists found Hizballah, an Islamic terrorist group bent on defeating the Israeli invaders and opposing their Western allies.

1983
April 18: A Hizballah suicide bomber kills sixty people and destroys the U.S. embassy in Beirut, Lebanon; two more suicide attacks against American targets in Lebanon follow over the next year and a half.

September: Under international criticism and pressure from the Israeli people, Israel's government orders a partial withdrawal from Lebanon.

1985
June: Leading a more moderate government, Prime Minister Shimon Peres orders a complete Israeli evacuation of Lebanon.

1987
December 8: Palestinian teenagers throw stones at Israeli forces and trigger the first intifada, a popular uprising against Israeli occupation.

1988
January: Arab fundamentalists establish the Hamas Islamic Brotherhood, an organization dedicated to destroying Israel.

November 15: The PNC recognizes Israel as a state; Arafat and the PNC declare an independent Palestine state in absentia and open talks with the United States.

1993
September: Under the Oslo Declaration of Principles, Israel and Palestine recognize each other's sovereignty; Israel grants PNC (now the Palestinian National Authority, or PNA) authority over select regions of Palestine; the PLO renounces terrorism and relocates its headquarters to Gaza, one of the two regions (the other is the West Bank) that remain under Israeli control.

1994
Hamas initiates its ongoing strategy of suicide bombings and other attacks upon targets inside Israel; Israel and Jordan sign a peace treaty.

1995
November 4: Israeli prime minister Yitzhak Rabin is assassinated by a right-wing Jewish extremist who believes Rabin's government is betraying Israel.

2000
May: Israel completes its full withdrawal from Lebanon; Hizballah guerrillas still harass Israel forces along the border.

July: Despite the pressures of the international community, Israeli prime minister Ehud Barak and PNA chief Arafat fail to reach a final peace agreement at Camp David in the United States.

September: Ariel Sharon, the conservative opposition leader in the Knesset, visits the Temple Mount in Jerusalem; because the site is also sacred to Muslims, Palestinians consider the visit a gesture of bad faith; violence ensues and conflict in the area continues through the early years of the twenty-first century; hundreds of Israelis and thousands of Palestinians die in the fighting.

2001
February 6: Ariel Sharon is elected prime minister of Israel; despite his conservative Likud Party leanings, he promises to work toward peace in the region.

September 11: In the wake of al Qaeda attacks on the World

Trade Center in New York, Israel and Palestine agree to a cease-fire, but it is never enforced.

2002
March: In response to increased suicide bombings, Israeli forces crack down on the PNA in the West Bank; Arafat, besieged in his compound in Ramallah, communicates to the outside world by telephone, airing his views that the Israelis have sabotaged the peace process by this act of aggression; the Israelis lose sympathy in the international community and call off the siege in May.

June: U.S. president George W. Bush calls for the creation of a Palestinian state after the PNA first puts new leadership in place; Israel reclaims all of the West Bank except Jericho.

2003
January: At a conference in Cairo, Egypt, Palestinian leaders disagree over a permanent cease-fire with Israel; the more conservative Islamic members insist that the PLO no longer voices the opinion of the majority of Palestinians who, supposedly, remain opposed to peace with Israel.

March 10: Arafat suggests to a PLO council that a prime minister should be elected to placate U.S. demands for new PNA leadership; the council appoints Abu Mazen, who some Westerners fear is a puppet of Arafat's, to the new post in April; Israel backs Mazen's appointment; Arafat quickly regrets his decision when Mazen refuses to follow orders.

March 19: A U.S.-led coalition invades Iraq; the United Nations' newly released "road map" to peace is allowed to languish by both the Israelis and the Palestinians.

June 4: Israeli prime minister Ariel Sharon and Abu Mazen hold the Aqaba Summit in Jordan to discuss implementing the "road map."

September 6: Mazen resigns as prime minister; two days later, Arafat and the PNA select Abu Ala (Ahmed Qurei) as prime minister.

September 10: After two suicide bombings that kill fifteen Israelis, the Israeli military again moves against Arafat's Ramallah headquarters.

October 5: The Israeli air force attacks bases in Syria allegedly used to train Palestinian terrorists.

October 9: Abu Ala tries to resign as the Palestinian prime minister over differences of opinion concerning the composition of his cabinet; the PNA rejects his decision, and Ala continues to form a government that pledges peace in Palestine.

For Further Research

MICHAEL BRECHER AND BENJAMIN GEIST, *Decisions in Crisis: Israel, 1967 and 1973*. Berkeley: University of California Press, 1980.

AHRON BREGMAN AND JIHAN EL-TAHRI, *Israel and the Arab: An Eyewitness Account of War and Peace in the Middle East*. New York: TV Books, 1998.

THOMAS A. BRYSON, *American Diplomatic Relations with the Middle East, 1784–1975: A Survey*. Metuchen, NJ: Scarecrow, 1977.

JIMMY CARTER, *Blood of Abraham*. Boston: Houghton Mifflin, 1985.

ELIAS CHACOUR, *We Belong to the Land*. San Francisco: Harper, 1990.

CHARLES ENDERLIN, *Shattered Dreams: The Failure of the Peace Process in the Middle East, 1995–2002*. Trans. Susan Fairfield. New York: Other Press, 2003.

ELIZABETH FERNEA, *The Struggle for Peace: Israelis and Palestinians*. Austin: University of Texas Press, 1992.

GLENN FRANKEL, *Beyond the Promised Land*. New York: Simon and Schuster, 1996.

MARTIN GILBERT, *Israel: A History*. New York: Morrow, 1998.

RASHID KHALIDI, *Palestinian Identity*. New York: Columbia University Press, 1997.

FRED J. KHOURI, *The Arab-Israeli Dilemma*. Syracuse, NY: Syracuse University Press, 1968.

BARUCH KIMMERLING AND JOEL S. MIGDAL, *The Palestinian*

People: A History. Cambridge, MA: Harvard University Press, 2003.

WALTER LAQUER AND BARRY RUBIN, *The Israel-Arab Reader*. New York: Penguin, 1995.

BERNARD LEWIS, *The Middle East: A Brief History of the Last 2,000 Years*. New York: Touchstone Books, 1997.

IAN LUSTICK, *Arabs in a Jewish State*. Austin: University of Texas Press, 1980.

BENNY MORRIS, *Righteous Victims: A History of the Zionist-Arab Conflict 1881–1999*. New York: Knopf, 1999.

MICHAEL OREN, *Six Days of War: June 1967 and the Making of the Modern Middle East*. New York: Oxford University Press, 2002.

AMOS OZ, *In the Land of Israel*. New York: Harcourt, Brace, Jovanovich, 1983.

WILLIAM B. QUANDT, *Peace Process: American Diplomacy and the Arab-Israeli Conflict Since 1967*. Washington, DC: Brookings Institution, 2001.

ITAMAR RABINOVICH, *Waging Peace: Israel and the Arabs at the End of the Century*. New York: Farrar, Straus and Giroux, 1999.

EDWARD SAID, *The Question of Palestine*. New York: Vintage, 1980.

URI SAVIR, *The Process: 1,100 Days That Changed the Middle East*. New York: Random House, 1998.

CHARLES E. SMITH, *Palestine and the Arab-Israeli Conflict*. 3rd ed. New York: St. Martin's, 1992.

SAMMY SMOOHA, *Israel: Pluralism and Conflict*. Berkeley: University of California Press, 1978.

MARK A. TESSLER, *A History of the Israeli-Palestinian Conflict*. Bloomington: Indiana University Press, 1994.

SHABTAI TEVETH, *Ben-Gurion and the Palestinian Arabs: From Peace to War*. New York: Oxford University Press, 1985.

BERNARD WASSERSTEIN, *Divided Jerusalem: The Struggle for the Holy City*. New Haven, CT: Yale University Press, 2001.

Index

DATE DUE

FOLLETT